# THE BRITISH & IRISH LIONS
## *On This Day*

# THE BRITISH & IRISH LIONS
## *On This Day*

SINCE 1888

*History, Facts & Figures*
*from Every Day of the Year*

**TIM EVERSHED**

# THE BRITISH & IRISH LIONS

## *On This Day*

### *History, Facts & Figures from Every Day of the Year*

*All statistics, facts and figures are correct as of 1st July 2016*

© Tim Evershed

Tim Evershed has asserted his rights in accordance with the Copyright, Designs and Patents Act 1988 to be identified as the author of this work.

Published By:
Pitch Publishing (Brighton) Ltd
A2 Yeoman Gate
Yeoman Way
Durrington
BN13 3QZ

Email: info@pitchpublishing.co.uk
Web: www.pitchpublishing.co.uk

Published 2016
Reprint 2019

A catalogue record for this book is available from the British Library

ISBN 9781785312045

Typesetting and origination by Pitch Publishing
Printed in India by Replika Press Pvt. Ltd.

## DEDICATION

To all those who have played with pride for
The British & Irish Lions.

# FOREWORD

It is always interesting, when reading a book such as this, to be reminded of the incredible story of the Lions. For me, the Lions are a remarkable phenomenon, with personal and collective reminders of unique and special rugby adventures.

The facts associated with the Lions are varied and unique and to read them presented in association with dates gives a real flavour of the Lions experience.

Going back in Lions' history it is amazing that the early tours exceeded six months with 30, or more, games. Sometimes speaking to today's players they are astonished to hear of being away from home for four months and playing in excess of 26 games.

To wear a Lions badge is very special because each Tour becomes very personal to that group of players, they define it, but the badge links them to its incredible history, not just events, but characters as well.

In a sense, the Lions are even bigger now than they have ever been, with huge support from four countries being prepared to travel halfway around the world in their thousands to be part of it. More than ever, the current Lions' tours share those special occasions with all the supporters who are so proud to follow the badge and have an association with it.

The Lions mean so much to so many more people that is something of which we should be incredibly proud. Having had the privilege to go on seven Lions' tours, I became even more convinced of the uniqueness of the experience. My last words as a Lions coach to a group of Lions players, in 2009, was, "When people look at you and the Lions badge, they will think good." May it always be.

This book is a reminder of the history and uniqueness of the Lions.

*Sir Ian McGeechan, OBE*

# ACKNOWLEDGEMENTS

I was fortunate that during the writing of this book I was able to call upon the many works of the historians and journalists that have recorded the story of the British & Irish Lions. The work of Clem Thomas, Greg Thomas, John Griffiths, Richard Bath and Rhodri Davies as well as a host of newspaper reports have also proved invaluable and my thanks go to all who have documented events so faithfully.

My thanks also go to Mick Lane, Allan Gray, Lee Grooby, Mark Hoskins, George and Pauline MacMillan, David Sherwood, Tim Clark, Dick Williams, Peter Wynne-Thomas and the staff of Radcliffe-on-Trent Library for their assistance.

I am indebted to my proofing team of Ruth Cassidy, David Evershed, Darryl Smith, Lawrence Telford and Susie Wyeth for their diligent efforts.

Once again my wife Hayley has provided love, support, patience and editing skills towards this book for which I'm truly grateful. Last, but certainly not least, thanks to my boys William and Joseph for their love and enthusiasm.

# INTRODUCTION

*The British & Irish Lions On This Day* chronicles the team's history in terms of the facts, figures and trivia that have occurred on each day of the calendar year.

When I began researching this book I already knew that The British & Irish Lions was a remarkable rugby team, one that counted the very best players from the Home Nations amongst its alumni. However, the sheer volume of eventful Tour stories, noteworthy matches and extraordinary individuals that are associated with the Lions story came as something of a surprise.

Since the first Tour in 1888 the Lions have created a unique touring history as a team while the players have led many interesting and successful lives on and off the rugby pitch.

Anyone reading this book from start to finish will be fed that history in a seemingly random and haphazard manner as it zips back and forth throughout the years. Nevertheless, I have endeavoured to include the important events and key characters that have shaped the Lions story. I also hope that there is more than a smattering of interesting anecdotes and enlightening tales for Lions fans everywhere.

Happy reading,

*Tim Evershed*

# THE BRITISH & IRISH LIONS
## *On This Day*

SINCE 1888

# JANUARY

## TUESDAY 1st JANUARY 1895

Andrew Stoddart, who captained The British & Irish Lions during the pioneering 1888 Tour, scored 173 in the second Ashes Test at the Melbourne Cricket Ground. Stoddart had ended the second day of the match unbeaten on 151 and added another 23 runs the following morning before being bowled by George Giffen. It was his highest score in Test cricket and was enough to give England a match winning lead that put his side 2-0 up in the series. Although the Australians rallied, taking the next two matches to level the series, Stoddart led his side to victory in the deciding fifth Test to win the Ashes. Stoddart was one of the outstanding players on the 1888 Tour to Australia and New Zealand and took over the captaincy following the tragic death of Robert Seddon.

## WEDNESDAY 1st JANUARY 1913

Basil Nicholson was born in London, England. The centre toured South Africa with the 1938 Lions winning a cap in the third Test in Port Elizabeth. Nicholson played in 10 matches on the Tour and scored two tries in the 45-11 victory over Rhodesia in Salisbury. After the outbreak of World War Two Nicholson was commissioned in the Royal Engineers and he played an active role in planning the D-Day landings in Normandy.

## MONDAY 2nd JANUARY 1956

Theodore Pike was knighted in the New Year's Honours List. The Irish prop toured Argentina with the 'Forgotten Lions' of 1927, playing in the first Test of the series. He went on to serve in the colonial administration and was Commissioner of British Somaliland between 1954 and 1959.

## TUESDAY 3rd JANUARY 1882

Johnnie Williams was born in Whitchurch, Wales. In 1906 the wing was first capped for Wales against South Africa and, despite losing in two of his first three games for his country, ended his international career with 15 victories from 17 caps. Williams scored 17 tries for Wales and helped the team complete three Triple Crowns. In 1908 he toured Australasia with Arthur 'Boxer' Harding's Anglo-Welsh side and was the leading try scorer with 12 scores in 19 matches.

## SATURDAY 4th JANUARY 1936

Prince Alexander Obolensky scored two tries as England defeated the All Blacks for the first time. The meeting at Twickenham was the third between the two teams and the hosts ran out 13-0 winners. Obolensky's first try, which saw him beat several defenders in a 70-metre run, is still rated as one of the finest ever scored by an England player. Obolensky was selected to tour Argentina with the 1936 Lions.

## FRIDAY 4th JANUARY 2013

England and Lions utility back Austin Healey appeared on *Celebrity Mastermind*. Healey, who toured twice with the Lions in 1997 and 2001, was up against TV presenters Nick Hancock and Michael Underwood as well as T'Pau singer Carol Decker. His specialist subject was Everton FC.

## WEDNESDAY 5th JANUARY 1955

Douglas Marsden-Jones died in London, England aged 61. The Welsh forward won two caps for his country and was called up to tour South Africa with the Lions in 1924. Marsden-Jones played in 12 matches on the Tour including two Tests.

## MONDAY 5th JANUARY 1970

*A Question of Sport* was shown nationally on BBC Television for the first time with Cliff Morgan as one of the original team captains. David Vine hosted the programme and boxer Henry Cooper captained the opposing side. Morgan played all four Tests of the 1955 series in South Africa and scored three points. Following his retirement from rugby he pursued a successful career as a broadcaster on radio and television.

## SATURDAY 6th JANUARY 1945

Barry John was born in Cefneithin, Wales. The Welsh fly-half was dubbed 'The King' by the New Zealand press for his starring role in the victorious 1971 series. John played in 17 matches on that Tour and scored 194 points including a full house of try, conversion, penalty and dropped goal against Waikato. He played in all four Tests against the All Blacks and his 30 points were vital in achieving the Lions' only series victory in New Zealand.

## SUNDAY 6th JANUARY 1974

Major General Sir Douglas Kendrew stood down as Governor of Western Australia. The former England and Lions prop, who was known as Joe in his time as a rugby player, was a highly decorated soldier who won the Distinguished Service Order four times. He toured New Zealand and Australia with the 1930 Lions playing in 11 Tour matches and scoring a try against Southland.

## THURSDAY 7th JANUARY 1965

Notorious London gangsters Ronnie and Reggie Kray were arrested and charged with running a protection racket in London. The twins went on trial the following March. Presiding over the trial, which ended with the jury unable to reach an agreement, was the Recorder of London Carl Aarvold. In 1927 Aarvold, who played on the wing, went on one of the 'Forgotten Lions' Tours to Argentina scoring eight tries in four internationals. Three years later he toured New Zealand and Australia with an official Lions party winning five Test caps and scoring another three international tries.

## MONDAY 8th JANUARY 1923

South African-born wing Stan Harris broke his leg while playing for an England XV in the final trial for that year's Five Nations Championship. For a time the injury looked to have ended Harris' rugby career and he took up ballroom dancing, winning the waltz section of the World Amateur Championships in London. A sporting all-rounder, Harris then went on to win the South African light-heavyweight title and returned to rugby with the Johannesburg-based club Pirates. He turned down a place in South Africa's Olympic boxing team in order to join the Lions on their 1924 Tour.

## SATURDAY 9th JANUARY 1909

Bristol lock Percy Down won his one and only cap as England took on Australia at the Rectory Field in Blackheath. It was the first meeting between the two countries and the Wallabies came out on top 9-3. A year earlier Down toured Australasia with the Lions playing in 21 of the 26 matches. He literally made a splash on the trip when he fell into Auckland harbour from the boat as the Lions departed for Australia.

## TUESDAY 9th JANUARY 1917

Haydn Tanner was born in Penclawdd, Wales. The scrum-half was still a schoolboy when he made his mark on the world of rugby by helping Swansea beat the touring All Blacks in 1935. He made his Welsh debut against New Zealand later that year and was on the winning side once again. Tanner toured South Africa with the 1938 Lions playing in 10 matches, including the second Test, and scoring a try against Orange Free State County.

## SATURDAY 10th JANUARY 1885

Schoolboy Willie Thomas made his Wales debut in a Home Championship match against Scotland at Hamilton Crescent in Glasgow whilst still a pupil at Llandovery College. The forward helped Wales earn a 0-0 draw and won another 10 caps for his country. Thomas toured New Zealand and Australia with the original Lions in 1888. He featured in 28 matches on the trip and scored two tries.

## SATURDAY 11th JANUARY 1890

Arthur Paul played the first of his two matches in goal for Blackburn Rovers. Rovers went down 3-2 at West Bromwich Albion in a Football League fixture and a week later beat Sunderland 4-2 in the first round of the FA Cup with Paul between the posts. Although Rovers progressed in the Cup, Paul's two appearances had cost five goals and he was quickly replaced. One commentator noted: "Whilst there was no doubting his temperament, his actual goalkeeping technique left much to be desired." Paul was a sporting all-rounder who toured Australia and New Zealand with the Shaw and Shrewsbury team in 1888 as well as enjoying a successful cricketing career with Lancashire.

## SATURDAY 12th JANUARY 1957

Ken Scotland marked his international debut by scoring all the points in the match. The full-back kicked a penalty and a dropped goal to help Scotland to a 6-0 win over the French in Paris during the 1957 Five Nations Championship. Scotland played in 22 matches, including five Tests, of 1959's Lions Tour to Australia and New Zealand scoring 72 points from 12 tries, six conversions, five dropped goals and three penalties.

## MONDAY 13th JANUARY 1919

*The London Gazette* announced the award of a second bar on the Military Cross of Charles Timms. The citation reads: "For conspicuous gallantry and devotion to duty. During a counter-attack this officer went forward from battalion headquarters and effected several rescues of seriously wounded men, conducting them personally through the lines. Throughout the week's fighting he worked day and night, and the manner in which he disposed of stretcher cases under heavy fire was admirable." In all, Timms was awarded the Military Cross four times, one of only four soldiers to have achieved this feat. The Australian-born centre studied medicine in Edinburgh and toured South Africa with the 1910 Lions. He followed in the footsteps of his brother Alec who also attended university in Scotland and returned to his home country with the 1899 Lions.

## MONDAY 14th JANUARY 1991

Mako Vunipola was born in Wellington, New Zealand. The prop was born into a Tongan rugby dynasty with his father, uncles and cousins all playing internationally for the island. Vunipola was raised in Wales and educated at Millfield School in England – which has produced a number of British & Irish Lions including Gareth Edwards and JPR Williams – and qualified for England on grounds of residency. He was selected for the 2013 Tour and featured in all three Tests.

## SATURDAY 15th JANUARY 1910

Flanker Charles 'Cherry' Pillman made his international debut as England celebrated the opening match at the new Twickenham Stadium with a first win over Wales in 12 years. There were 18,000 people at the ground's opening match to see England win 11-6 thanks to scores from Fred Chapman and Barney Solomon. Tom Evans and Reggie Gibbs, a veteran of the 1908 Lions Tour, touched down for the Welsh. The Wales side also featured Jack Jones who had also toured Australasia two years earlier and would travel to South Africa with the 1910 side later that year. He was joined by Welsh teammate Harry Jarman as well as Pillman, who was one of the stars of the Tour and played a vital role in the second Test victory.

## SATURDAY 15th JANUARY 1977

Welsh lock Geoff Wheel and Irish Number Eight Willie Duggan became the first players ever to be sent off in a Five Nations match. Wheel threw a punch in Wales' 25-9 win in Cardiff and Duggan retaliated so both men received their marching orders. Despite this incident they were both selected for the Lions Tour of New Zealand later in the year. Duggan featured in 15 matches, including all four Tests, and was a major reason for the tourists' forward superiority over the All Blacks. However, Wheel was forced to withdraw from the squad after being diagnosed with a heart condition.

## WEDNESDAY 16th JANUARY 1907

Alfred Shaw died in Nottingham, England aged 64. Shaw was best known as a cricketer and was one of the finest bowlers of the Victorian era taking over 2,000 wickets in a career that spanned four decades. Shaw was a member of England's first ever Test match line-up and was a pioneer of overseas cricket Tours going to North America and Australia. In 1888 he and his Nottinghamshire and England teammate Arthur Shrewsbury decided to promote a rugby tour to Australasia that has retrospectively been recognised as the first British & Irish Lions Tour.

## TUESDAY 17th JANUARY 1961

Michael Kiernan was born in Cork, Ireland. The centre, who is the nephew of 1968 Lions captain Tom Kiernan, won his first Ireland cap in 1982 and gained a total of 43 during an international career that lasted nine years. In 1983 he played in all three Test matches as well as seven other fixtures in New Zealand. He scored two tries for the Lions and kicked a dropped goal.

## WEDNESDAY 17th JANUARY 1996

British & Irish Lions and Scotland full-back Gavin Hastings was the guest on ITV's *This is Your Life*. Michael Aspel, with his famous red book, took Hastings by surprise at Murrayfield shortly after his retirement from rugby. Hastings captained the Lions in New Zealand in 1993 and was part of the triumphant trip to Australia three years earlier. In all, he played 17 times for the Lions and scored 170 points.

## WEDNESDAY 18th JANUARY 1888

The Rugby Football Union issued a statement following Arthur Shrewsbury and Alfred Shaw's request for approval for a Tour of Australia and New Zealand, it said: "The rugby union committee wish it to be known that in response to the request from the promoters to give their support and approval to the projected football Tour to Australia they declined to do so. They do not consider it within their province to forbid players joining the undertaking but they feel it their duty to let gentlemen who may be thinking of going know that they must be careful in any arrangements made that they do not transgress the laws for the prevention of professionalism. The committee will look with a jealous eye upon any infringement of such laws, and they desire specially to call attention to the fact that players must not be compensated for loss of time."

## SATURDAY 18th JANUARY 1958

Wales had a late chance to win their Five Nations match against England, but Terry Davies' long-range penalty attempt into the wind at Twickenham rebounded off the crossbar to leave the scores locked at 3-3. That night a group of Welsh supporters climbed the posts and cut down a section of the offending crossbar and took it back to Wales. Davies, a timber merchant by trade, later offered to replace the missing woodwork. The following year the full-back toured New Zealand with the Lions winning two Test caps and kicking five points.

## FRIDAY 19th JANUARY 1968

The Reverend Robin Roe's award of the Military Cross after distinguishing himself for bravery during the Aden Emergency was announced in *The London Gazette*. The citation reads: "Oblivious to the heavy fire being directed at the camp, he attempted to drive about 400 yards across open desert to the scene of an accident... He was turned back forcibly by another officer only after he had personally been shot at and his Land Rover hit by machine gun fire." Roe, an Irish hooker with a 20-inch neck, toured South Africa with the 1955 Lions. He played in 11 Tour matches scoring a try against Griqualand West and packing down in the front row against Eastern Province despite suffering from two cracked ribs.

ALFRED SHAW

## SATURDAY 20th JANUARY 1900

Cardiff captain Gwyn Nicholls returned to action for the club in a 14-0 victory over Bristol after missing the first 19 matches of the season. The centre had only returned to the Welsh capital nine days earlier having stayed on in Australia following the previous summer's Lions Tour. Nicholls, who was the first Welshman to play a Lions Test, had been one of the stars of the Tour scoring 12 tries in 18 matches. Two of his try haul came in the Test series, which the Lions won 3-1. Instead of returning home immediately after the Tour Nicholls elected to work in a Brisbane bank leaving Cardiff in ignorance of their skipper's whereabouts. On his eventual return he was welcomed back by both club and country and after just one appearance for Cardiff he faced Scotland the following Saturday.

## SATURDAY 20th JANUARY 1934

Cecil Pedlow was born in Lurgan, Northern Ireland. A sporting all-rounder, Pedlow played tennis in the Junior Wimbledon championships and represented Ireland at both squash and rugby. At home at either centre or wing, he scored 31 points in 30 matches for Ireland and was selected to tour South Africa with the Lions in 1955. The 21-year-old Pedlow played in 13 matches on the Tour, including two Tests, and scored 58 points from eight tries, 11 conversions and four penalties.

## WEDNESDAY 20th JANUARY 1965

Queen Elizabeth II appointed England wing Carl Aarvold, who toured with the Lions in 1927 and 1930, as a Lieutenant of the City of London.

## SATURDAY 20th JANUARY 1973

Tom Grace's injury time try at Lansdowne Road levelled the scores at 10-10 between Ireland and New Zealand. Ireland fly-half Barry McGann missed the conversion and the match finished in a draw, which is the only time Ireland have avoided defeat to the All Blacks. The following year Grace toured South Africa with the Lions scoring 13 tries in 11 matches on the wing. He scored a hat-trick against the African XV and four tries against Griqualand West.

## SATURDAY 21st JANUARY 1911

Newport full-back Stanley Williams made his international debut for England against Wales after a tug-of-war between the two countries over his eligibility. Williams won three England caps before retiring from international rugby at the end of the Five Nations. The previous year the still uncapped Williams had toured South Africa with the Lions scoring four tries in 16 matches and playing in all three Tests.

## SATURDAY 22nd JANUARY 1955

Wales centre Bleddyn Williams, one of the stars of the 1950 Lions Tour, led his country to a 3-0 victory over England in the opening fixture of the Five Nations Championship. Alongside Williams, in a Welsh team that would go on to share the title with France, were a number of his teammates from the trip to Australasia, including Ken Jones and Rex Willis. The side that beat England also featured a number of players bound for South Africa on the 1955 Tour including Cliff Morgan and Bryn Meredith.

## MONDAY 23rd JANUARY 1933

Arthur Smith was born in Castle Douglas, Scotland. The wing captained both Scotland and the British & Irish Lions during his career. He made his Scotland debut in February 1955 and toured South Africa with the Lions later in the year. Injuries restricted Smith to five matches on the trip but he still managed nine tries including five in the 39-12 win over East Africa on the way home. He returned to South Africa seven years later as Lions captain, scoring another eight tries in 14 appearances. However, his side lost the Test series 3-0 with one match drawn.

## SATURDAY 24th JANUARY 1925

Scotland wing Ian Smith scored four tries as France were thrashed 25-4 at Inverleith. Smith had toured South Africa with the Lions the previous year scoring five tries in just six appearances. Making his Scotland debut in the match, which put the Scots on course for their first ever Grand Slam, was David MacMyn. The lock ended on the winning side in 10 of his 11 matches for his country and captained the 1927 Lions to a 4-0 series victory in Argentina.

## TUESDAY 25th JANUARY 1927

Osbert Mackie died in Redcar, England aged 57. The centre scored 10 tries and a dropped goal in 15 matches of the 1896 Tour of South Africa. He was selected for all four Tests in a series the Lions won 3-1. Originally a member of Wakefield Trinity Mackie resigned the captaincy of the club when it went professional in the great schism of 1895 that saw the formation of rugby league.

## THURSDAY 26th JANUARY 1871

In response to a letter from Edwin Ash, the representatives of 21 rugby clubs met at the Pall Mall restaurant in London and formed the Rugby Football Union. Ash's letter said: "Those who play the rugby-type game should meet to form a code of practice as various clubs play to rules which differ from others, which makes the game difficult to play." Ash later managed the 1891 Tour to South Africa, which was the first trip to go ahead with the RFU's blessing.

## FRIDAY 26th JANUARY 1990

John Robbie hosted his first current affairs show on the South African radio station Talk Radio 702. The scrum-half won nine caps with his native Ireland and joined the 1980 Lions in South Africa after being called up as injury cover. He played in seven matches, including the consolation victory in the final Test, and scored a try in the 23-19 win over Griqualand West.

## SATURDAY 27th JANUARY 1973

A Barbarians side featuring 14 British & Irish Lions, plus the uncapped Englishman Robert Wilkinson, beat New Zealand 23-11 in one of the most memorable matches of rugby ever played. The match at Cardiff Arms Park was billed as a rematch after the victorious Lions Tour of 1971. It opened with one of the greatest tries of all time, scored by scrum-half Gareth Edwards. The move began near the Baa-Baas own goal line with Phil Bennett evading three tacklers using his famous sidestep. The ball passed through the hands of JPR Williams, John Pullin, John Dawes, Tom David and Derek Quinnell before Edwards arrived out of nowhere to dive in at the corner.

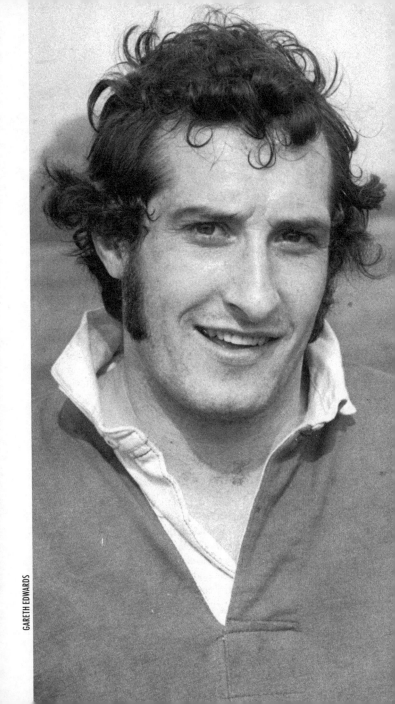

GARETH EDWARDS

## MONDAY 28th JANUARY 1889

Phil Waller was born in Bath, England. Although born in England, Waller played his rugby over the border for Monmouthshire and Newport. The forward went on to win six caps for Wales before travelling to South Africa as one of the record seven Newport players selected for the 1910 Lions. Waller played in 23 of the 24 matches on the Tour and kicked one penalty. He stayed on in South Africa at the end of the Tour before joining the South African Artillery Regiment at the outbreak of World War One and was killed in action near Arras, France in 1917.

## SATURDAY 29th JANUARY 1977

1966 tourist David Watkins coached the Wales rugby league team to a 6-2 victory over England at Headingly in Leeds. Later that year Watkins would guide Great Britain to the World Cup final where they lost by a point to Australia. Prior to his conversion to rugby league the fly-half had won 21 caps for Wales and six for the British Lions, captaining the tourists in two Tests of the 1966 series against New Zealand.

## FRIDAY 30th JANUARY 2015

Cardiff, Wales and British & Irish Lions prop Howard Norris died in Cardiff aged 80. Norris toured Australia and New Zealand with the 1966 Lions playing 17 matches, kicking three conversions and winning three Test caps, one more than he gained for Wales. In a long domestic career Norris clocked up 415 first team appearances for Cardiff, which remains the club record.

## SUNDAY 31st JANUARY 1937

England lock Brian Black won a gold medal as one half of the British two-man bobsleigh team at the World Championships at Cortina in Italy. South African-born Black was one of the stars of the 1930 Tour to New Zealand and Australia. He played in 20 matches including all five Tests. Although he was a second row Black was one of the best goal kickers of the era and 65 of his 77 points on Tour came from the boot, including six conversions in the 33-9 win over Otago.

# THE BRITISH & IRISH LIONS
## *On This Day*

SINCE 1888

# FEBRUARY

## SATURDAY 1st FEBRUARY 1958

Wing Peter Jackson scored one of the all-time great tries as England staged a late comeback to beat Australia 9-6 at Twickenham. Wales and Lions fly-half Cliff Morgan rated the score as one of his top five tries of all-time, he said: "Five minutes to go and the Australians seemingly had the match won... quick hands from Jeeps and Butterfield to Jackson on the wing. He had the Australian cover to beat; there was no space. Jackson handed off Phelps, shaped to come inside Curley, then opted for the outside again and sped for the corner... genius at work." Jackson scored 19 tries in just 18 matches of the 1959 Tour, including two four-try hauls and a hat-trick.

## SATURDAY 2nd FEBRUARY 1952

1950 Lions scrum-half Rex Willis played with a broken jaw for the last 30 minutes of Wales' Five Nations clash with Scotland at Cardiff Arms Park. The Welsh won the match 11-0 thanks to a try from wing Ken Jones, another 1950 Lion, which was converted by centre Malcolm Thomas. Thomas, who toured with the Lions in 1950 and 1959, added two penalties as Wales headed for their fifth Grand Slam and 12th championship title.

## SATURDAY 2nd FEBRUARY 1974

The Old brothers, Alan and Chris, represented England at rugby union and cricket, respectively, on the same day. Fly-half Alan was part of the England team that beat Scotland 16-14 at Murrayfield while fast bowler Chris took the field against the West Indies in Trinidad. Alan went on to tour South Africa with the Lions later in the year. He played in four matches scoring 59 points, including a record 37 in the thrashing of South Western Districts. Old was expected to provide Phil Bennett with competition for the Test jersey but his Tour was cut short by a serious leg injury.

## TUESDAY 3rd FEBRUARY 1942

Scotland and Lions wing Roy Kinnear collapsed and died while playing rugby for the RAF in Uxbridge, England. The centre toured South Africa with Ronald Cove-Smith's Lions in 1924 playing in all four Tests and six other matches.

## SATURDAY 3rd FEBRUARY 1951

Scotland's Number Eight Peter Kinnimonth kicked an unlikely dropped goal to set the home side on their way to a shock 19-0 win over Wales in Edinburgh. The Welsh side featured 11 of the 1950 Lions and were heavy favourites but were blown away in the second half after Kinnimonth, the only veteran of the previous Lions Tour in the Scottish ranks, had put Scotland 3-0 up at half-time. BBC commentator Bill McLaren said: "Wales had 11 British Lions in that side so that Scotland's triumph held out some promise for the future. Instead Scotland lost those next 17 internationals in which they scored just 11 tries and conceded 51."

## SATURDAY 4th FEBRUARY 1933

Scotland wing Ian Smith scored his 24th and final international try in an 11-3 Home Nations Championship victory at St Helens in Swansea. His total of 24 tries remained a world record for over 50 years until broken by Australian wing David Campese in 1987. Smith captained Scotland to the Triple Crown in his final season of international rugby. He toured South Africa with the 1924 Lions playing six matches, including two Tests, and scoring five tries.

## TUESDAY 4th FEBRUARY 1936

Andy Mulligan was born in Kasauli, India. The Irish scrum-half was called up as an injury replacement for the New Zealand leg of the 1959 Tour. Mulligan played in 13 matches on Tour, including the fourth Test victory against the All Blacks.

## SATURDAY 4th FEBRUARY 1961

The British & Irish Lions were well represented as the Barbarians inflicted the only defeat of South Africa's European Tour. The Springboks had completed the Grand Slam with victories over all four home nations but went down 6-0 at Cardiff Arms Park. It was the Baa-Baas' first win over South Africa with Wales and Lions flanker Haydn Morgan scoring one of the tries and England international Derek Morgan getting the other. 1959 skipper Ronnie Dawson joined a number of past or future Lions including, Tony O'Reilly, Syd Millar, Richard Sharp, Roddy Evans and Brian Price, in the victorious Barbarians team.

## SATURDAY 5th FEBRUARY 1955

Wing Arthur Smith touched down as Scotland broke a 17-match losing streak with a 14-8 victory over Wales at Murrayfield in the Five Nations Championship. Scotland had failed to win a match since beating the Welsh four years earlier, a miserable run that had included a record 44-0 defeat at the hands of the Springboks. Smith toured South Africa twice with the Lions scoring 17 tries in 19 matches, including five against East Africa on the 1955 Tour, and captained the team seven years later.

## WEDNESDAY 5th FEBRUARY 1992

Director Louis Malle's film *Damage* was released in the UK. It starred Jeremy Irons as a doctor and government minister who conducts an ill-fated affair with his son's fiancée, who was played by Juliette Binoche. Welsh centre Ray Gravell, who toured South Africa with the Lions in 1980, played the role of Irons' chauffeur in the film.

## SATURDAY 6th FEBRUARY 1971

Welsh flanker John Taylor kicked "the greatest conversion since St Paul" to seal a dramatic late victory over Scotland at Murrayfield. Wales trailed until Gerald Davies' try in the corner had closed the gap to a single point. With normal kicker Barry John suffering from concussion Taylor stepped up to add the extras from the touchline to keep Wales' quest for a sixth Grand Slam on track. Taylor toured with the 1971 Lions playing 15 matches including all four Tests and scored four tries.

## SATURDAY 7th FEBRUARY 1891

Wing Paul Clauss scored two tries on his Scotland debut as Wales were beaten 15-0 at Raeburn Place in Edinburgh. Clauss went on to enjoy a successful Home Championship scoring a try against Ireland and a dropped goal versus England as the Scots clinched their first Triple Crown and third title overall. Later in the year Clauss joined the 1891 Lions in South Africa. His Tour got off to a blistering start with tries in the first four matches. Clauss appeared to enjoy the trip off the pitch too, describing it in his diary as all "champagne and travel".

## SATURDAY 8th FEBRUARY 1964

Mike Gibson made his Ireland debut at the age of 21 in an 18-5 win over England at Twickenham. It was the start of a record-breaking Test career with both his country and the British & Irish Lions. The fourth most capped Lion with 12 Tests, he was the most capped player in world rugby at the time of his international retirement in 1979 with 81. Teammate Syd Millar said: "One of the finest players of his generation, one of the finest players ever to represent Ireland and the British & Irish Lions and a man who epitomised the very ethos of the game and its values."

## SATURDAY 8th FEBRUARY 1964

All Black captain Wilson Whineray became the first rugby player to appear on BBC Radio's *Desert Island Discs*. Whineray, who led New Zealand to a 3-1 victory over the British Lions in 1959, included music by George Handel, Giuseppe Verdi and Ella Fitzgerald among his selections and asked for a guitar as a luxury item.

## SUNDAY 9th FEBRUARY 1964

Dewi Morris was born in Crickhowell, Wales. The scrum-half made his England debut in 1988 against Australia and went on to win 29 caps playing a part in two Grand Slam sides and helping England to a third-place finish in the 1995 World Cup. He toured New Zealand with Gavin Hastings' Lions side in 1993 playing in eight matches, including all three Tests.

## SATURDAY 10th FEBRUARY 1962

Ireland lock Willie John McBride made his international debut in a 16-0 Five Nations loss to England at Twickenham. The match marked the start of a 13-year Test career that saw McBride win 63 Ireland caps as well as a record 17 for the British & Irish Lions. Amongst McBride's other Lions records are his five Tours, jointly held with compatriot Mike Gibson, and his 70 appearances in a Lions shirt. McBride was appointed captain for his fifth and final Tour in 1974 and led an unbeaten side through South Africa making it the most successful Lions trip of modern times.

## SATURDAY 10th FEBRUARY 1973

Following his side's 18-9 loss to Ireland at Lansdowne Road the England captain John Pullin joked, "we might not be any good but at least we turned up". Scotland and Wales had refused to travel to Ireland due to fears over security with the Troubles at their height. England had surprisingly agreed to play but performed poorly in Dublin. Pullin toured twice with the Lions, in 1968 and 1971, playing 27 times including seven Test matches.

## SATURDAY 11th FEBRUARY 1911

Irish prop Dr Tommy Smyth scored the only points of the game with a try as Ireland narrowly beat England 3-0 in Dublin in the Five Nations. The previous summer Smyth had led the Lions on their fourth Tour of South Africa. Smyth was the first Irishman to captain the Lions and one of a record seven Newport players on the Tour. Although the series was lost 2-1 Smyth won much praise for his leadership of the party. He played in 18 matches on Tour, including two Tests, featuring in almost every forward position and scoring five tries.

## SATURDAY 12th FEBRUARY 1949

Fergus Slattery was born in Dun Laoghaire, Ireland. The flanker's international career spanned 14 seasons with Ireland and two Tours with the British & Irish Lions. He first toured with the 1971 Lions featuring in 14 non-international matches. He gained selection again three years later and was a key member of the undefeated team in South Africa. Slattery played in all four Tests and if his try in the final Test had not been controversially ruled out, the Lions would have boasted a 100% record. Later he led Ireland on its most successful Tour of Australia and took part in the 1982 Triple Crown-winning side.

## FRIDAY 13th FEBRUARY 1874

Frederick Belson was born in Ramsgate, England. The forward played club rugby for Clifton, Bath, Bristol and Abergavenny but never won an England cap. However, he was invited to join the Reverend Matthew Mullineux's team on the 1899 Tour of Australia. Belson made seven appearances for the Lions including playing in the first Test defeat.

## SATURDAY 13th FEBRUARY 1937

Lions lock Brian Black added gold in the four-man bobsleigh World Championships to the one he took in the two-man event the previous month. The British team, led by FJ McEvoy, beat off the challenge of the Germans and Americans at St Moritz to take the title. The team had an aggregate time of five minutes and 8.5 seconds for four runs. Black toured New Zealand and Australia in 1930 scoring four tries for the Lions. He served as a Pilot Officer in the RAF during World War Two and was killed in action during the Battle of Britain in July 1940.

## SATURDAY 14th FEBRUARY 1970

Ireland wing Tony O'Reilly won his final cap 15 years and 23 days after he had made his debut as a teenager. O'Reilly's call-up was a major surprise coming seven years after his last appearance for Ireland but he couldn't prevent the team going down 9-3 to England at Twickenham. O'Reilly toured twice with the Lions and holds the record for tries scored with 38 in 38 matches. He won 10 Test caps for the tourists and scored six tries in international matches.

## SUNDAY 15th FEBRUARY 1942

The island of Singapore fell to the Japanese in World War Two. Amongst those taken as a Prisoner of War by the Japanese was 1924 tourist Stan Harris. Harris was promoted to Lieutenant-Colonel and appointed senior officer in command of F Force, a forced labour party of 7,000 prisoners. Harris is known to have stood up for his men but despite his efforts they suffered appalling conditions and high casualties, as they were force-marched to work areas on the Burmese railway.

## SUNDAY 15th FEBRUARY 2004

Prop Jason Leonard made his 114th and final England appearance as Italy were thrashed 50-9 at the Stadio Flaminio in Rome. Leonard retired from international rugby with 119 caps in all, five for the Lions, as the most capped player – a record that has since been broken. Leonard's international career spanned 14 years, three Lions Tours, two World Cup finals, including the 2003 victory, and four England Grand Slams.

## WEDNESDAY 16th FEBRUARY 1921

Bob Evans was born in Rhymney, Wales. The flanker played for Newport and Monmouthshire before making his Welsh debut against France in 1947. He was selected to tour Australasia with the 1950 Lions winning six Test caps. In total he played in 17 matches on the Tour and scored two tries.

## THURSDAY 17th FEBRUARY 1955

Walter Carey died in Eastbourne, England aged 79. The forward toured South Africa with the Lions in 1896 playing 17 matches. He scored a try in the first Test against the Springboks and another in the 26-3 victory over Port Elizabeth. Carey was an Oxford educated priest who served as a Military Chaplain during World War One. In 1921 he returned to South Africa and was appointed Bishop of Bloemfontein.

## MONDAY 18th FEBRUARY 1963

Rob Andrew was born in Richmond, North Yorkshire, England. The England fly-half twice toured with the Lions as well as having the honour of captaining the side in the 1989 match against France that marked the Bicentennial of the French Revolution. Andrew played a key role in the 1989 series victory and helped run New Zealand close three years later. In all he appeared 13 times for the Lions scoring 40 points.

## SATURDAY 19th FEBRUARY 1881

England's Harry Vassall scored the first hat-trick in a rugby international, as Wales were thrashed 8-0 at Blackheath. The match was Wales' first ever international and a scratch side were not even given the chance to train together before playing. Vassall was a key figure in the development of English rugby and was one of the selectors for the first officially sanctioned Lions Tour of South Africa in 1891.

## SATURDAY 20th FEBRUARY 1982

Fly-half Ollie Campbell scored all 21 of his side's points as Ireland sealed their fifth Triple Crown with a 21-12 win over Scotland. A prolific goal kicker, Campbell scored 184 points for the Lions over Tours of South Africa in 1980 and New Zealand three years later.

## WEDNESDAY 21st FEBRUARY 1917

Charles Gregory Wade stood down as the Member of New South Wales Parliament for Gordon after 13 years service. The Australian had won three rugby Blues while studying at Oxford University in the 1880s and went on to win eight England caps scoring seven tries, including a hat-trick against Wales. He never finished on the losing side for either Oxford or England. On his return to Australia he faced the 1888 Lions as part of the Past and Present XV of King's School, Parramatta that held the original tourists to a draw. He was knighted in 1918 and made a Knight Commander of the Order of St Michael and St John two years later.

## THURSDAY 22nd FEBRUARY 1923

Bleddyn Williams was born in Taff's Well, Wales. Known as 'The Prince of Centres' Williams was acknowledged as the best midfielder in Britain in the late 1940s and early 1950s. Together with Jack Matthews he formed a formidable centre partnership for Cardiff, Wales and the 1950 British & Irish Lions. Williams was renowned for his hard tackling and deceptive running style. He played in 21 matches on the 1950 Tour captaining the team in three of his five Test matches.

## SATURDAY 23rd FEBRUARY 1884

Angus Stuart, one of the 1888 tourists, was part of the four-man threequarter line pioneered by Cardiff in a match at Gloucester. At the time rugby was played with nine forwards and six backs. The system proved a success for Cardiff and was copied by Wales three years later. The seven backs and eight forwards formation became accepted worldwide and is used in rugby union to the present day.

## WEDNESDAY 24th FEBRUARY 2010

Trevor Ringland was selected to stand in the UK's General Election as a joint candidate for the Ulster Unionist Party and the Conservatives in East Belfast. Ringland came third in the poll three months later receiving 7,305 votes. Ringland played nine times for the 1983 Lions as well as appearing for the team in a match celebrating the IRB's centenary three years later.

## SUNDAY 25th FEBRUARY 1945

Gilbert Collett died in Huddlecote, England aged 65. The wing won rugby Blues at Cambridge University before going on to play for Cheltenham, Gloucestershire and the Barbarians. Although never selected to play for England he was chosen to tour South Africa with the British Isles in 1903. Collett enjoyed a fantastic start to the Tour dropping a goal in the opening game and scoring eight tries in his first 11 fixtures.

## SUNDAY 26th FEBRUARY 2012

England and Lions hooker Brian Moore was the guest on BBC Radio's *Desert Island Discs*. Moore's music choices included songs by Genesis, Pink Floyd and The Stranglers while he asked to take Emile Zola's *Germinal* as his book on the island. Moore is one of seven Lions to have appeared on *Desert Island Discs*.

## FRIDAY 27th FEBRUARY 1942

Irish full-back Cecil Boyd died in Victoria, British Columbia, Canada aged 66. Boyd toured South Africa with the 1896 Lions playing in the 8-0 first Test victory at Port Elizabeth. Although he was dropped for the rest of the Test series, Boyd managed 11 more appearances in a Lions shirt. A qualified doctor, he served with the Royal Army Medical Corps in World War One winning the Military Cross. The citation reads: "He repeatedly attended to wounded under heavy shell fire, and on several occasions was compelled to evacuate his aid post, succeeding each time in removing all his wounded."

## THURSDAY 28th FEBRUARY 1974

Clem Thomas stood as the Liberal Party's candidate for the constituency of Gower in the 1974 UK General Election. Thomas polled 8,737 votes equating to 19.3% of the vote as Labour comfortably held on to a safe seat. The flanker won 26 caps for Wales between 1949 and 1959. He toured South Africa with the 1955 Lions, and despite missing the first 10 games of the Tour because of appendicitis, played in 10 matches, including two Tests, and captained the team in the 11-8 win over Natal. After retiring from rugby Thomas covered the sport as a journalist and wrote a comprehensive history of the Lions.

# THE BRITISH & IRISH LIONS
## *On This Day*

SINCE 1888

# MARCH

## SATURDAY 1st MARCH 1924

Louis Greig was appointed as Gentleman Usher to the Royal Household. Greig was a friend and mentor to Prince Albert, who became King George VI. The two had served together in the Royal Navy and partnered each other in the Men's Doubles at Wimbledon in 1926. Greig also played a crucial role in the prince's courtship with Lady Elizabeth Bowes-Lyon. The Scotland wing toured South Africa with Jonny Hammond's 1903 Lions playing in 17 matches including all three Tests.

## SUNDAY 1st MARCH 1953

Sir Louis Greig died in Ham, Surrey aged 72. The 1903 tourist lived one of the most colourful lives of any Lion. A royal confidante, Royal Navy and Royal Air Force surgeon, prisoner of war during World War One and a sportsman. Greig was knighted after helping Ramsay MacDonald form the National Government in 1931. The Scotsman's funeral was attended by representatives of five of the most senior members of the Royal family, Winston Churchill, J. Arthur Rank, the Scottish rugby team and six waiters from the Dorchester Hotel. Greig's finest moment in a Lions shirt came when he scored two tries in a 28-7 victory over Grahamstown.

## SATURDAY 1st MARCH 1980

An unfortunate error in the programme for France's Five Nations clash with Ireland in Paris saw the first letter of Colm Tucker's surname replaced with an 'F'. The mistake was compounded as the stadium announcer repeated it when the Irish flanker entered the fray as a replacement. Later that year Tucker toured South Africa with the Lions featuring in the final two Tests of the series as well as seven Tour matches.

## MONDAY 2nd MARCH 1908

Welsh wing Reggie Gibbs scored four tries as France were trounced 36-4 in Cardiff in the first ever meeting between the two nations. Although France had not officially joined the Home Championships, the victory is usually now combined with the Welsh Triple Crown that season and is considered the first Grand Slam. Gibbs was selected to tour Australasia with the Lions playing in two Tests. In total he scored 13 tries and kicked 28 points in 16 Lions matches.

## WEDNESDAY 2nd MARCH 1927

Ray Prosser was born in Pontypool, Wales. A reluctant tourist who feared flying, the prop nevertheless played in 13 matches of the 1959 Tour of Australia and New Zealand. Prosser was on the winning side in all but one of his Lions matches scoring a try against Manawatu and earning selection for the final Test against New Zealand, which was won 9-6. After retiring from playing Prosser coached his hometown club to two Welsh titles and played a major role in the development of players such as Bobby Windsor, Charlie Faulkner, Graham Price, Terry Cobner and Staff Jones who all earned caps for both Wales and the Lions in the 1970s and 1980s.

## TUESDAY 3rd MARCH 2015

Wellington College won the McEvedy Shield for a record 49th time. In 1922 New Zealand-born Lion Pat McEvedy donated the trophy to serve as the prize for the winners of an annual athletics competition that is held for four schools in the Wellington area of New Zealand. Despite never gaining an international cap for either England or New Zealand McEvedy twice toured with the Lions. He visited Australia and New Zealand in 1904, and 1908, whilst training to be a doctor at Guy's Hospital in London where he played for the rugby team. In total he appeared in 31 Lions matches scoring seven tries and kicking two conversions. He returned to New Zealand in later life and served as President of the NZRFU in 1934 and 1935.

## MONDAY 4th MARCH 1878

Bill MacLagan made his Scotland debut at full-back, in a scoreless draw with England in a Home Nations international at Kennington Oval in London. The player would go on to win a record 25 caps for Scotland playing most of his international rugby at threequarter. He retired from international rugby after a loss to England in 1890. However, the following year he was persuaded to captain the first official Lions Tour to South Africa. The 33-year-old MacLagan played in 19 out of the 20 Tour matches, including three Tests, scoring eight tries. The 1891 tourists won all of their matches and are the only Lions team to boast a 100% record on Tour.

## SUNDAY 4th MARCH 1906

Tommy Jones-Davies was born in Nantgaredig, Wales. The centre made his Wales debut against England in the 1930 Five Nations and was selected to join the Lions in Australia and New Zealand later that year. On Tour he scored an impressive 11 tries from 12 non-international matches, including a hat-trick against West Coast/Buller, but was not selected for the Test team. Two four-point dropped goals brought his points total for the Lions to 41.

## SATURDAY 5th MARCH 1892

1891 tourist William Bromet scored a try as England beat Scotland 5-0 to clinch their third Triple Crown in the Home Championship. Also part of the England side that triumphed at Raeburn Place was 1888 tourist Tom Kent. England won the title in impressive fashion with 29 points scored and none conceded over three matches.

## SATURDAY 5th MARCH 1977

Welsh fly-half Phil Bennett inspired his team to a 14-9 victory over England in the Five Nations Championship with a famous pre-match speech. He said: "Look what these bastards have done to Wales. They've taken our coal, our water, our steel. They buy our homes and live in them for a fortnight every year. What have they given us? Absolutely nothing. We've been exploited, raped, controlled and punished by the English - and that's who you are playing this afternoon." Later that year Bennett would captain a British & Irish Lions squad that included six Englishmen on its Tour of New Zealand.

## SATURDAY 5th MARCH 1988

Back row forwards John Jeffrey and Dean Richards took the Calcutta Cup for a drunken kick about on Princes Street following England's 9-6 win over Scotland at Murrayfield. The cup, which was more than a century old, was damaged in the incident. Jeffrey received a six-month ban from the Scottish Rugby Union while Richards only got a month from the RFU. The two forwards were teammates on the 1989 Lions Tour to Australia.

## WEDNESDAY 6th MARCH 1895

Andrew Stoddart's England cricket XI retained the Ashes with a six-wicket win at the Melbourne Cricket Ground. As well as captaining England at cricket Stoddart, also captained the Barbarians, England and the 1888 Lions at rugby.

## FRIDAY 6th MARCH 2015

Wales and Lions Number Eight Scott Quinnell appeared on the Sky 1 comedy *Stella* alongside actress Ruth Jones. Quinnell twice toured with the Lions with his first trip to South Africa in 1997 cut short after just three games by a double hernia operation. Four years later he went to Australia and played in all three Test matches. A try in the first Test added to the hat-trick he had scored in the opening match of the Tour against Western Australia.

## THURSDAY 7th MARCH 1974

England and Lions hooker Peter Wheeler scored a hat-trick of tries on his Barbarians debut as the East Midlands were thrashed 40-7. It was the first of 17 appearances the Leicester front-rower would make for the Baa-Baas. He also went on to win 41 England caps as well as seven for the Lions over two Tours in 1977 and 1980.

## SATURDAY 8th MARCH 2014

Ireland and British Lions centre Brian O'Driscoll became the most capped player in rugby union history when he made his 140th international appearance as his country thrashed Italy 46-7 in the Six Nations. O'Driscoll won his 141st and final cap the following week as Ireland clinched the championship with a 22-20 victory over France in Paris. O'Driscoll was selected for four Lions Tours scoring a spectacular debut try and being named captain for the ill-fated 2005 Tour of New Zealand.

## FRIDAY 9th MARCH 1888

The 1888 tourists departed Tilbury docks for New Zealand on the SS *Kaikoura* following a send-off dinner at the Manchester Hotel in London the previous evening. A 46-day journey saw stops in Plymouth, Tenerife, Cape Town and Hobart before they finally arrived in Dunedin on 22nd April and opened their Tour seven days later.

## MONDAY 9th MARCH 1970

Martin Johnson was born in Solihull, England. The second row first won international recognition for New Zealand's Under-21 side while playing two seasons for King Country. After returning to his native country he won a first England cap in 1993 and toured New Zealand with the Lions later that year. Four years later he was a surprise selection to lead the tourists to South Africa where his side beat the world champions 2-1 in the Test series. Johnson became the first man to captain two Lions Tours when he took charge again in Australia in 2001 and two years later he lifted the Webb Ellis Trophy as England's World Cup winning captain. In all he played in eight Lions Tests, captaining the side in six of those, and a further seven Tour matches.

## MONDAY 10th MARCH 1879

England and Scotland played for the Calcutta Cup for the first time. The eighth match between the two sides took place at Raeburn Place in Edinburgh and ended in a 1-1 draw with the home side scoring a dropped goal while England kicked a goal. Playing at full-back for the Scots was Bill MacLagan who would go on to captain both his country and the 1891 Lions on the team's first ever Tour of South Africa.

## SUNDAY 10th MARCH 1957

Terry Holmes was born in Cardiff, Wales. The scrum-half was twice selected for the Lions and both times saw his Tour cut short by injury, managing just four games on each trip. Despite playing in only eight matches for the tourists, Holmes still managed to score four tries.

## SATURDAY 11th MARCH 1911

1908 Lion Reggie Gibbs and 1910 tourist Jim Webb both scored as Wales completed the first Grand Slam since France had officially joined the Five Nations championship, with a 16-0 win over Ireland in Cardiff. Wing Johnnie Williams, who had toured Australasia with Gibbs three years earlier, was also a member of the winning Welsh team.

## TUESDAY 12th MARCH 1907

Robert Kelly was born in Edinburgh, Scotland. The centre toured Argentina on one of the Lions' 'Forgotten Tours' to South America in 1927. The Tour was a success with all nine matches won, including all four internationals against the Pumas. Kelly played in three of the four internationals matches and scored five tries against Argentina.

## MONDAY 12th MARCH 1973

Willie Llewellyn died in Pontyclun, Wales aged 95. The wing was the last surviving member of the Wales team that had beaten the Original All Blacks 3-0 in 1905. In 1904 Llewellyn toured with the Lions scoring a try in each of the three Test victories over Australia as well as appearing in the defeat to New Zealand. In all he played in 13 matches on the Tour scoring six tries.

## TUESDAY 13th MARCH 1888

Cecil Rhodes launched the De Beers Consolidated Mines company with £200,000 of capital. Rhodes was named chairman of the new company, which went on to dominate the world diamond trade and his financial guarantee enabled the second ever Lions Tour, the first to South Africa, to go ahead. "Let them come. I shall stand firm for any shortfall," said Rhodes.

## SATURDAY 13th MARCH 1948

Ireland secured their first ever Grand Slam with a 6-3 victory over Wales in front of 32,000 at Ravenhill. Hooker Karl Mullen captained Ireland to the title and two years later was chosen to lead the first post-war Lions Tour to Australasia. Also on the pitch in Belfast were Jackie Kyle, Bill McKay, Jimmy Nelson and Jim McCarthy who all joined Mullen.

## SATURDAY 14th MARCH 1896

Five future Lions were in the Ireland side that beat Wales 8-4 in Belfast to seal their second Home Nations Championship title. Forward Tom Crean scored a try and Lawrence Bulger kicked a conversion in the match. The pair would head to South Africa with the Lions later that year and were joined by teammates Andrew Clinch, Louis Magee and Jim Sealy.

## THURSDAY 15th MARCH 1877

The first ever cricket Test began at the Melbourne Cricket Ground with Australia taking on England. England's first Test captain was James Lillywhite, who was one of the managers of the Lions' 1888 Tour while his co-manager, Alfred Shaw, bowled the first ever ball in Test cricket.

## WEDNESDAY 15th MARCH 1916

*The London Gazette* announced that Frank Stout, who captained the Lions in three Tests of the 1899 series in Australia, had been awarded the Military Cross for "conspicuous gallantry and resource." The citation reads: "On hearing that a number of the enemy were working close to the British lines Stout... took Corporal Tester and a light machine gun to a saphead. The corporal stood on the lieutenant's back and opened fire on the enemy. He fired 150 rounds while exposed to a heavy return fire, and then got down to allow Second-Lieutenant Stout to mount and open fire in turn. Next morning fourteen of the enemy's dead were counted."

## SATURDAY 15th MARCH 1975

Ireland centre Dick Milliken won his last cap as the side went down 32-4 in Cardiff. A double break of leg and ankle later in the year effectively ended Milliken's international career. He had won his first cap two years earlier becoming the first player from the Bangor club in Northern Ireland to represent Ireland. Although he was usually regarded as the junior partner to Ireland great Mike Gibson, it was Milliken who in 1974 played all four Tests alongside Ian McGeechan in midfield.

## WEDNESDAY 16th MARCH 1870

Walter Jackson was born in Gloucester, England. Aged 21, the forward was chosen to join the first officially sanctioned Lions Tour to South Africa in 1891. Jackson played in five matches of the Tour without scoring any points. He earned one England cap in 1894, when he was played out of position on the wing, and became a rugby league player the following year when his club Halifax joined the fledgling Northern Union.

## SUNDAY 17th MARCH 1940

Jim Telfer was born in Melrose, Scotland. The Number Eight made his name with his hometown rugby club before winning 25 Scotland caps and touring with the Lions in 1962 and 1966. He coached the Lions in 1983 and Scotland to a Grand Slam the following year. Telfer was also Ian McGeechan's assistant coach on the successful 1997 Tour becoming noted for his stirring pre-match orations that players said had the "hairs on the back of the neck standing up".

## MONDAY 17th MARCH 1980

Bill Beaumont was named as captain of the Lions squad that was selected to tour South Africa that summer. The lock had led England to their eighth Grand Slam with a 30-15 victory over Scotland two days earlier. Welsh Number Eight Derek Quinnell had not played for his country during the Five Nations but was selected to make his third Lions Tour. Also making their third Tours were England prop Fran Cotton and Scotland full-back Andy Irvine.

## FRIDAY 18th MARCH 1938

Tour Manager Major Bernard Hartley announced the squad for the 1938 Tour of South Africa. Ireland and Instonians prop Sam Walker was selected as captain for the trip but it was omissions like English hooker Henry Toft and the Welsh duo of Cliff Jones and Wilf Wooller that stood out. English journalist Teddy Wakelem wrote: "Through business and other reasons we are unable to send out the real, full force of our rugger representation… in fact one could write down a representative team of those staying behind."

## MONDAY 18th MARCH 1968

Ireland's Tom Kiernan was named as Lions captain for the 1968 Tour of South Africa. Joining the full-back were his countrymen Syd Millar and Willie John McBride, who were on their third Lions Tours. Mike Gibson, Jim Telfer, Delme Thomas and Sandy Hinshelwood were all named for a second Tour. Kiernan played in 13 matches on the Tour kicking 84 points including all but three of the Lions' Test points in a 3-0 series defeat to the Springboks.

## SATURDAY 19th MARCH 1983

Irish fly-half Ollie Campbell had a personal points haul of 21 - from a try, conversion and five penalties - as Ireland beat England 25-15 to take a share of the Five Nations title. It took Campbell's tally for the championship to 52 points, which set a new record for the tournament. The fly-half was also a prolific scorer for the Lions, kicking 24 conversions, 35 penalties and nine dropped goals over two Tours.

## MONDAY 19th MARCH 2001

Gordon Brown died in Troon, Scotland aged 53. The second row, who was nicknamed "Broon frae Troon", toured three times with the Lions during the 1970s forging a formidable partnership with Willie John McBride on the first two of those. Rugby writer Richard Bath said: "A buoyant larger-than-life figure, Brown was an abrasive steamroller of a lock... he also displayed a dynamism in the loose and an ability to look after himself when the going got tough." Brown played in eight Tests and 33 other Tour matches for the Lions scoring nine tries.

## SATURDAY 20th MARCH 1909

Frank Handford won the last of his four England caps in an 18-8 defeat to Scotland at the Athletic Ground in Richmond. The following year the forward was selected to tour South Africa with the Lions under the captaincy of Tommy Smyth. Handford played in 18 matches on the Tour, including all three Tests, and scored a try in the 30-10 victory over Border Bulldogs in East London.

## SATURDAY 21st MARCH 1903

Centre Alec Timms kicked a dropped goal to help Scotland beat England 10-6 at the Athletic Ground in Richmond. The victory sealed the Scots' fourth Triple Crown and sixth Home Championship title overall. Australian-born Timms had toured the country of his birth with the Lions four years earlier scoring 11 tries in 15 appearances. The centre missed the first Test defeat but played the rest of the series scoring a try in the third Test as the Lions came back to take the series 3-1. His younger brother Charles was also a Lion who toured South Africa in 1910.

## SATURDAY 21st MARCH 1925

A Scotland side containing five British & Irish Lions completed the country's first ever Grand Slam by beating England 14-11 at Murrayfield. England had won the Grand Slam in the preceding two seasons and the defeat was their first Five Nations loss in 12 matches. Scotland full-back Dan Drysdale, wing Ian Smith, Herbert Waddell and Number Eight Doug Davies had all toured South Africa with the Lions in 1924, while lock David MacMyn would captain the 1927 Tour of Argentina.

## MONDAY 22nd MARCH 1971

Wales' Grand Slam in the Five Nations was rewarded when a Lions squad containing 13 Welshman was announced for the trip to New Zealand. Unsurprisingly, the choices for coach and captain were also Welshman Carwyn James and John Dawes, respectively. As well as a host of star names from Wales' title winning team, including Barry John, Mervyn Davies, JPR Williams and Gareth Edwards, the squad contained two uncapped players. Llanelli Number Eight Derek Quinnell and Harlequins flanker Peter Dixon were yet to play for their countries although the latter won his first England cap before the Tour departed.

## THURSDAY 22nd MARCH 1984

The choir of King's House School, including a 12-year-old Lawrence Dallaglio, sang at the wedding of composer Andrew Lloyd-Webber and singer Sarah Brightman. The following year the choir went on to provide backing vocals for Tina Turner's hit *We Don't Need Another Hero*. Dallaglio, who captained England and toured three times with the Lions, said: "It was a very enjoyable part of my life. As well as singing for Tina Turner, I got to sing at Andrew Lloyd Webber's wedding. People have visions of choristers in gowns, but that was never my experience. I'm very proud of that period in my life."

## FRIDAY 23rd MARCH 1945

King George VI appointed Tommy Vile to the position of High Sheriff of Monmouthshire. Vile had toured Australia and New Zealand under the captaincy of David Bedell-Sivright in 1904 winning three Test caps.

## TUESDAY 24th MARCH 1885

England cricket captain Arthur Shrewsbury scored his maiden Test century in the fifth and deciding Ashes Test at the Melbourne Cricket Ground. Shrewsbury scored 105 not out to help set up an England win by an innings and 99 runs that clinched the series 3-2. Shrewsbury, along with fellow England cricketers Alfred Shaw and James Lillywhite, pioneered Tours in both his own sport and in rugby.

## SATURDAY 24th MARCH 1945

Operation Varsity was launched involving more than 16,000 paratroopers and several thousand aircraft. It was the largest airborne operation in history to be conducted on a single day and in one location. Amongst those taking part was glider pilot Bleddyn Williams. Known as the "Prince of Centres", he toured Australasia with the Lions in 1950. He played three Tests against New Zealand, captaining the side in two of them, and another two against Australia where he scored a try in the 19-6 first Test victory in Brisbane.

## SATURDAY 25th MARCH 1950

There were 12 players bound that year's Lions Tour on the pitch in Cardiff as Wales clinched their fourth Grand Slam - and first for 39 years - with a convincing 21-0 victory over France. Future Lions Ken Jones, Jack Matthews and Roy John all scored tries while Lewis Jones, who was called up as an injury replacement for the Tour, kicked nine points.

## SATURDAY 26th MARCH 1949

Wales and Lions hooker William 'Bunner' Travers won his final Welsh cap 12 years after he had first represented his country at the age of 35. Travers is one of only a handful of players to win international caps either side of World War Two. He had first played for Wales in 1937 and toured South Africa with the Lions the following year. Despite missing the first Test through injury, Travers made the most appearances on the Tour with 21 and scored one try against Natal.

## SATURDAY 26th MARCH 1966

Wales wing Stuart Watkins ran 70 yards down the touchline to score a match – and championship – winning interception try against France in Cardiff. The spectacular score not only clinched the Five Nations title for the Welsh but also assured Watkins of selection for the upcoming Lions Tour to Australasia. The wing played in 13 matches on the Tour, including both Tests against the Wallabies and the third Test against New Zealand. Watkins scored five tries against non-international opposition on the Tour.

## WEDNESDAY 26th MARCH 1975

Gordon Bulloch was born in Glasgow, Scotland. The hooker was first called up by the Lions in 2001 as an injury replacement for England's Phil Greening. He played in four matches on the Tour including an appearance from the bench in the first Test victory in Brisbane. Bulloch made another six appearances in New Zealand four years later. He captained the midweek side in three fixtures and when he was brought on in the third Test became the only Scot to play in a Test match on the 2005 Tour.

## THURSDAY 27th MARCH 1980

Roger Spong died in Surrey, England aged 73. The fly-half was selected to tour Australasia in 1930 and the England international was one of the stars of the Lions' back division, with the Australian press dubbing him 'Slippery Spong' and comparing him favourably to cricket great Don Bradman. Spong played in all five Tests and 12 further Tour matches scoring seven tries.

## SUNDAY 28th MARCH 1976

Swansea captain and Number Eight Mervyn Davies suffered a career ending brain haemorrhage while playing in a Welsh Cup semi-final match. Despite the loss of Davies, Swansea went on to win the match 22-14 against Pontypool before losing the final to Llanelli. Davies played 38 times for Wales and eight times for the Lions and was only on the losing side nine times. He played in two Welsh Grand Slam sides and toured with the Lions in 1971 and 1974. In all he played 27 matches over the two Tours and scored eight tries.

## SATURDAY 29th MARCH 1884

Queens Park became the first Scottish team to play in the FA Cup Final as they went down 2-1 to Blackburn Rovers in front of 12,000 at Kennington Oval. Four years later Queen's Park forward Dr John Smith would join the original Lions on their Tour of New Zealand and Australia as referee. Smith was primarily known as a Scottish football international, but he also played rugby for Edinburgh University and Edinburgh Wanderers and had been a reserve for the Scottish national rugby team.

## FRIDAY 29th MARCH 1940

Prince Alexander Obolensky died at RAF Martlesham Heath in Suffolk aged 24. The England wing, who had toured Argentina with the 1936 Lions, died when his Hawker Hurricane overshot the runway and crashed into a ravine breaking his neck.

## THURSDAY 30th MARCH 1950

The 1950 squad assembled at the Mayfair Hotel in London with Ireland hooker Karl Mullen leading the first Lions Tour for 12 years due to World War Two. Preparations for the trip to New Zealand included a dinner as guests of the New Zealand Society at the Savoy Hotel and photos at Twickenham before they departed by train from Euston Station for Liverpool where they boarded the *Ceramic*.

## TUESDAY 31st MARCH 1959

Moseley and England flanker Peter Robbins' Lions Tour was ended before the team had even departed when he suffered a broken leg representing the Barbarians in a 15-5 loss to Newport on the team's traditional Easter Tour of Wales. His injury sent shockwaves through the 1959 tourists. Irish wing Tony O'Reilly said: "After that we were afraid to cross the road, let alone take any serious exercise."

## SATURDAY 31st MARCH 1979

Rubistic, with jockey Maurice Barnes on board, won the Grand National at Aintree racecourse in Liverpool. The horse, which was the first Scottish trained winner of the famous steeplechase, was owned by John Douglas, who played in 10 provincial matches on the 1962 Lions Tour of South Africa.

# THE BRITISH & IRISH LIONS
## *On This Day*

SINCE 1888

# APRIL

## SATURDAY 1st APRIL 1939

Sam Walker's 1938 tourists reconvened to play an unofficial Lions match against their manager BC 'Jock' Hartley's XV at Ravenhill in Belfast. Although three of the 1938 tourists, Haydn Tanner, Stan Couchman and Ivor Williams appeared in the manager's back-row, the Lions won 39-12 scoring nine tries in the process.

## THURSDAY 1st APRIL 1948

John James Williams was born in Nantyffyllon, Wales. The wing, universally known by his initials JJ, toured twice with the Lions in the 1970s and is one of the side's greatest ever try scorers. He scored braces in back-to-back Tests against the Springboks in 1974 and those four tries tied countryman Willie Llewellyn for the most scored by a Lion in a single series. Williams added another Test try in New Zealand three years later and his total of five is behind only Tony O'Reilly on the all-time list. In all Williams scored 22 tries in 26 Lions matches putting him third on the list for all matches, behind O'Reilly and Randolph Aston.

## TUESDAY 2nd APRIL 1912

German football club VfB Stuttgart was founded by the amalgamation of FV Stuttgart and Kronen-Klub Cannstatt at a meeting held at the Concordia Hotel in Cannstatt. VfB's predecessor clubs were both formed originally as rugby clubs following the introduction of the sport in the area by English expatriate William Cail in the 1860s. Cail went on to serve as president and treasurer of the RFU, playing a key role in the development of Twickenham, as well as coaching the 1910 Lions in South Africa.

## TUESDAY 3rd APRIL 1877

James Lillywhite took four wickets as England reduced Australia to 207 for seven in their second innings during the second ever cricket Test. Lillywhite finished with his Test best figures of four for 70 as England went on to win the match by four wickets at the Melbourne Cricket Ground. In 1888 he teamed up with two of his England cricket colleagues, Alfred Shaw and Arthur Shrewsbury, to promote the original Lions Tour.

## FRIDAY 3rd APRIL 1908

Arthur 'Boxer' Harding's Anglo-Welsh team departed from London bound for New Zealand and Australia on the *Athenic*. The side arrived in Wellington on 17th May and played 26 matches on the Tour winning 16, drawing one and losing nine. They lost the Test series 2-0 to the All Blacks, with a match drawn, but did not face the Wallabies on the Australian leg.

## FRIDAY 3rd APRIL 1936

Scotland and Lions forward Robert MacMillan died after a hunting accident while riding with the Earl of Bathurst's Hounds near Cirencester in Gloucestershire on his 71st birthday. The Wiltshire and Gloucestershire Standard reported: "In the neighbourhood of the Ewepens, in Cirencester Park, the hounds were in full cry after the first fox of the day. His horse refused a wall and Mr MacMillan was thrown over the wall, alighting on his head." MacMillan won 21 Scotland caps in a decade and went on the Lions' first Tour of South Africa in 1891. He played 20 matches on the Tour, including all three Tests, scoring three tries.

## MONDAY 4th APRIL 1988

Paul Dodge led Leicester to the inaugural Courage League title with a 39-15 victory over Waterloo at Welford Road. Dodge was called up as an injury replacement for the 1980 Tour of South Africa. He played in five of the last seven matches of the Tour, scoring a try against the Junior Springboks on his Lions debut. Dodge won two Lions caps and played a key part in the fourth Test victory at Loftus Versfeld in Pretoria.

## TUESDAY 5th APRIL 1853

Conservative MP Henry Goulburn introduced a bill in Parliament for "the future regulation, management, and permanent endowment of the College of Christ of Brecknock". Now known as Christ's College, Brecon the school has produced seven British & Irish Lions. The first two were Arthur Harding and Teddy Morgan who toured in 1904 and the most recent was 1983 Lion Robert Ackerman. Most impressively the school provided five tourists for the 1908 Tour including captain Harding, James Jones, Jack Jones, John Dyke and Willie Llewellyn.

## SATURDAY 5th APRIL 1879

John Smith scored his first international goal on his debut for Scotland's football team in a 5-4 loss to England at Kennington Oval in London. Smith went on to score 10 goals in 10 appearances for Scotland. Smith also played as a forward at rugby for Edinburgh University and Edinburgh Wanderers and although never capped by Scotland at the game he joined the 1888 Tour party. He acted as referee on the Tour as well as playing in nine matches.

## TUESDAY 6th APRIL 1926

Tom Elliott was born in Galashiels, Scotland. The prop was first capped for his country in the 1955 Five Nations Championship and was selected to join the Lions in South Africa later that year. Elliott made his Lions debut in the 32-6 win over Transvaal Universities and went on to play in a further seven non-international matches on the Tour.

## SATURDAY 7th APRIL 1888

Halifax beat Wakefield Trinity in the final of the Yorkshire Cup despite having to replay one of their earlier matches in the competition. The replay had been forced upon Halifax after opponents Dewsbury had accused them of fielding a "professionalised" player in one of the earlier rounds. The player in question, Jack Clowes, had received £15 in order to buy kit to go on the Lions' 1888 Tour. The RFU ordered a rematch, which Halifax won, while Clowes went on the Tour of Australia and New Zealand but played in no matches.

## TUESDAY 8th APRIL 1986

Alan Morley scored a try in Bristol's 30-0 thrashing of Exeter at the County Ground. It was the wing's final domestic score for Bristol on his way to a club record 384 tries. Morley also played, and scored tries, for Gloucestershire, the South West, the Barbarians, England and the Lions to accumulate a world record of 479 first class scores. Morley was selected to tour South Africa with the 1974 Lions playing in two non-international matches and scoring a try in the 56-10 victory over the African XV.

## SATURDAY 9th APRIL 1904

In preparation for the Tour later that year the RFU placed an advertisement in *The Times* newspaper that read: "As it has been decided that the Rugby Football team visiting Australia this summer shall also play matches in New Zealand, the committee think it desirable to add a number of forwards. Before making the final selection the committee wish to give other players, in the new circumstances, an opportunity of sending in their names if they wish to undertake the trip."

## MONDAY 9th APRIL 1945

Lieutenant Colonel Paddy Mayne of the SAS was awarded the Victoria Cross for his actions in leading two armoured jeep squadrons through the front lines toward Oldenburg, Germany in order to sow disorganisation amongst the enemy. Despite his "brilliant military leadership and cool calculating courage" the award was later downgraded to a third bar on his Distinguished Service Order. Mayne, who played 20 matches including all three Tests of the 1938 South African Tour, is one of only seven British servicemen to receive the DSO four times.

## SATURDAY 10th APRIL 1965

Lions full-back Tom Kiernan kicked two penalties to help Ireland to their first ever victory over South Africa. Ireland triumphed 9-6 at Lansdowne Road with wing Paddy McGrath scoring a try for the home side. Kiernan was one of 10 Lions in the Ireland side, including seven out of eight forwards. Mike Gibson, Roger Young, Ken Kennedy, Ray McLoughlin, Willie John McBride, Bill Mulcahy, Mick Doyle, Ronnie Lamont and Noel Murphy all toured with the Lions in the 1960s and 1970s.

## SATURDAY 10th APRIL 1999

Scotland and Lions fly-half Gregor Townsend became only the fifth man in the history of the Five Nations to score a try in every round of a tournament. Townsend touched down in a 36-22 win over France to help Scotland to the title. Also on the scoresheet in Paris was centre Alan Tait with a brace of tries. Both men had toured South Africa two years earlier, playing key roles in the Lions' series victory.

## FRIDAY 11th APRIL 1856

Arthur Shrewsbury was born in New Lenton, England. The Nottinghamshire and England cricketer was renowned as one of the greatest batsmen of his generation with many observers judging him the equal of WG Grace. He was the first Test cricketer to pass 1000 runs and domestically he topped the batting averages five times in the seven seasons from 1886 to 1892. In one of those seasons, 1888, he did not play in England as he was touring Australia and New Zealand, firstly as a cricketer and secondly as promoter and manger, along with Alfred Shaw and James Lillywhite, of the first Lions Tour.

## WEDNESDAY 12th APRIL 1950

The *Ceramic* docked in Curacao in the Dutch West Indies with the 1950 Lions party aboard. Two days later the ship entered the Panama Canal before crossing the Pacific Ocean and arriving in New Zealand on the 2nd May.

## SATURDAY 12th APRIL 1969

Lions wing Maurice Richards scored four tries as Wales thrashed England 30-9 in Cardiff to complete the Triple Crown and secure the Five Nations title. The Welsh had been denied a Grand Slam by a surprise draw with France, who had lost all three of their other matches, the previous month. Richards had toured South Africa with the 1968 Lions, playing in all three Test matches. The wing did not score in the internationals but managed five tries in his eight other Tour games.

## WEDNESDAY 13th APRIL 1910

*The Times* announced the original party for the 1910 Tour to South Africa. However, the squad suffered a number of withdrawals before departure the next month with seven of the original backs and two forwards pulling out. Established internationals who were unable to join the Tour included Welshmen Willie Morgan and Phil Hopkins, English backs Harry Shewring and Percy Lawrie, Scottish trio of James Pearson, Walter Sutherland and Louis Spiers as well as Irish full-back Billy Hinton. This left captain Dr Tom Smyth with an inexperienced squad containing eight players who would never be deemed good enough to win caps for their countries.

## SATURDAY 13th APRIL 1963

Ireland and Lions wing Tony O'Reilly scored both tries of the match as the Barbarians beat Cardiff 6-0 on their Easter Tour. The scores were O'Reilly's final ones for the Baa-Baas and took his tally to 38 for the club, which is a record. The wing's total of 30 appearances is also a Barbarians record.

## SATURDAY 14th APRIL 1979

Iain Balshaw was born in Blackburn, England. Balshaw made his England debut in 2000 and was selected to go on the Lions Tour of Australia the following year. He scored two tries in the Tour opener against Western Australia and appeared as a replacement in all three Tests.

## MONDAY 14th APRIL 2003

Bob Evans died in Abergavenny, Wales aged 82. The flanker was known for his defensive qualities with a combination of hard tackling and outstanding positional play that would help contain opposition fly-halves and disrupt midfields. He won 10 caps for Wales and travelled to Australasia with the 1950 Lions. Evans played in all six Tests on the Tour as well as 11 other matches and scored two tries.

## SUNDAY 15th APRIL 1945

Brigadier Glyn Hughes was the first Allied medical officer to enter the concentration camp at Bergen-Belsen following its liberation. Hughes took charge of the camp and later testified against camp Commandant Josef Kramer and others at their war crimes trial. Hughes had acted as referee on the Lions Tour to Argentina in 1936, the final Tour before the outbreak of World War Two.

## SATURDAY 15th APRIL 1967

Wales full-back Keith Jarrett scored 19 points, including a spectacular try when he returned a kick from his own 22, to mark his international debut at the age of just 18. Jarrett's haul included two penalties and five conversions as England were beaten 34-21 in Cardiff. The following year he toured South Africa with the Lions playing five non-international matches and scoring 18 points.

## WEDNESDAY 16th APRIL 1986

As part of the IRB's centenary celebrations the British Lions faced a Rest of the World team at Cardiff Arms Park. The Rest of the World side were 15-7 victors in the match, which was played in wet conditions. Australians Simon Poidevin and Nick Farr-Jones scored tries, which were both converted by Michael Lynagh who also added a penalty. The Lions' points came through a John Beattie try and a Gavin Hastings penalty. The match was the only one played by the 1986 Lions as the scheduled Tour of South Africa did not go ahead due to apartheid.

## WEDNESDAY 17th APRIL 1963

Damian Cronin was born in Wegberg, Germany. The second row won 45 Scotland caps over a ten-year international career and was part of the 1990 Grand Slam-winning team. Three years later Cronin was selected to tour New Zealand with Gavin Hastings' Lions. He played in six Tour matches and scored a try against Taranaki.

## SATURDAY 17th APRIL 1971

1971 tourist John Spencer captained England against a star-studded President's XV as part of the RFU's centenary celebrations at Twickenham. Full-back Bob Hiller, who was also bound for New Zealand with the Lions, scored all of England's points converting his own try from the touchline and adding two penalties. Despite his efforts the hosts went down 28-11 with All Black wing Bryan Williams scoring a hat-trick and Ian Kirkpatrick adding a brace, both men would face the Lions later in the year. Brian Lochore, who came out of retirement for the occasion, captained the President's XV. He had been the skipper of the victorious All Blacks on the Lions' 1966 Tour to New Zealand.

## SUNDAY 18th APRIL 1993

Lawrence Dallaglio scored a try and Nick Beal kicked three conversions as England beat Australia 21-17 to win the inaugural World Cup Sevens tournament. Also playing in the victorious English team was scrum-half Matt Dawson. The trio all went on to tour South Africa in 1997 with Dallaglio and Dawson both playing key roles in the Test series victory.

## WEDNESDAY 18th APRIL 2007

1980 tourist Ray Gravell was admitted to hospital with a diabetes-related infection that caused his right leg to be amputated below the knee. Despite the operation Gravell's health problems continued and he died of a heart attack six months later. The centre made his name with Llanelli before earning a first Welsh cap in 1975. In 1980 he toured South Africa with the Lions winning four Test caps and playing in seven other matches. He scored one try for the Lions in the 26-19 second Test defeat in Bloemfontein.

## TUESDAY 19th APRIL 1938

Derrick Grant was born in Hawick, Scotland. The flanker established himself as a Scottish international while playing for his hometown club. He toured New Zealand and Australia in 1966 under fellow Scot Mike Campbell-Lamerton, playing in 10 Tour matches.

## SATURDAY 20th APRIL 1895

Frank Stout played his final match for Gloucester City FC as the team brushed Trowbridge Town aside 4-0 in a Bristol & District League fixture. Stout scored two goals in 37 appearances for City and also toured twice with the Lions. The forward appeared 41 times for the tourists, setting a record that stood until the 1950s, playing in seven Test matches and scoring 26 points.

## WEDNESDAY 20th APRIL 2011

Dyson 'Tug' Wilson died in West Cornwall, England aged 84. The South African-born flanker won England caps while playing for the Metropolitan Police. Wilson played 15 non-international matches on the 1955 Lions Tour of his native country and scored tries against Boland, Western Province Universities and Natal.

## SUNDAY 21st APRIL 1912

Sam Walker was born in Belfast, Ireland. The front row forward captained the Lions on the 1938 Tour for South Africa, leading the team in 20 of their 24 matches on the trip including all three Test matches. Under his leadership the Lions were known for their exciting, attacking style and the team was rewarded with a stunning, upset win in the final Test against the Springboks.

## WEDNESDAY 21st APRIL 1915

England and Lions forward Alexander Todd died in Poperinge, Belgium aged 41. He had been seriously wounded in the assault on Hill 60 during the First Battle of Ypres a few days earlier. Todd was uncapped at the time of his selection for the 1896 Tour to South Africa. He played in 19 of the 21 matches and won a place in the side for all four Tests against the Springboks, scoring a try in the 17-8 victory in the second match of the rubber. Four years later he won his only England caps in the final two matches of that year's Home Championship.

## TUESDAY 21st APRIL 2009

At a press conference in the Sofitel hotel at Heathrow Airport, London, Ian McGeechan announced the 37-man squad that would take on the Springboks that summer. McGeechan, who was on his fourth Tour as Head Coach, selected Ireland second row Paul O'Connell as Lions captain for the trip.

## FRIDAY 22nd APRIL 1763

The Blakiston Baronetcy of the City of London was created in the Baronetage of Great Britain for Matthew Blakiston, who had been Lord Mayor of London from 1760 to 1761. His descendant Sir Arthur Blakiston inherited the title in 1941 becoming the 7th Baronet 17 years after he had joined the Lions on a Tour of South Africa playing four Tests against the Springboks.

## SUNDAY 22nd APRIL 1888

The SS *Kaikoura* docked at Port Chalmers, Dunedin carrying the first party of Lions on a Tour organised by cricketers Alfred Shaw and Arthur Shrewsbury. The Tour would last seven months and feature 35 rugby matches as well as 19 games of Victorian Rules football and a cricket match.

## SATURDAY 22nd APRIL 1939

Jock Brown, father of Gordon Brown – who toured three times with the British & Irish Lions in the 1970s – played in goal as Clyde beat Motherwell 4-0 to win the Scottish Cup for the first time in the club's history.

## SUNDAY 22nd APRIL 1990

England and Lions centre Will Carling scored two tries as a Four Home Unions XV beat a Rest of Europe XV at Twickenham. There were 10 more Lions in the home side, which was captained by David Sole and included Gavin Hastings, Jeremy Guscott, John Jeffrey and Peter Winterbottom. The match was played to raise funds for Romania following the overthrow of Communist dictator Nicolae Ceausescu.

## THURSDAY 23rd APRIL 1896

The first selection for the second Tour to South Africa was made at a meeting of the RFU at the Craven Hotel in London. The initial squad contained only 13 names and omitted any half backs. Englishmen Sydney Bell and the Reverend Matthew Mullineux were added later as was Ireland's Louis Magee. England forward Johnny Hammond, a veteran of the 1891 Tour, captained the final squad with Froude Hancock also making a second Tour. The large Irish contingent included Magee's brother James, Thomas Crean and Robert Johnston.

## WEDNESDAY 24th APRIL 1974

Former Scotland and Lions fly-half Gordon Waddell was elected to the South African Parliament by winning the constituency of Johannesburg North for the Progressive Party. Waddell was one of seven new Progressive Party MPs who won election in 1974 and supported Helen Suzman who had been the sole anti-apartheid MP for 13 years. Waddell toured New Zealand with the Lions in 1959 and South Africa three years later. He won two Test caps against the Springboks and played in 22 matches overall scoring 41 points for the tourists.

## SATURDAY 24th APRIL 1976

Coach Carwyn James led Llanelli to their fourth Welsh Cup victory in succession as Swansea were beaten 16-4 at Cardiff Arms Park. Under James' guidance the club monopolised the competition in its early years finishing runners up to Neath in the first edition in 1972 before winning the next four finals. Cardiff were beaten in 1973 before victories over Aberavon in the two following seasons. James revolutionised rugby union coaching in Wales and beyond as he masterminded the Lions' sole Test series victory in New Zealand in 1971.

## SUNDAY 25th APRIL 1915

Major Blair Swannell was killed in action during the Gallipoli campaign in World War One. Serving with the 1st Battalion of the Australian Imperial Force he was in one of the first groups to land at Anzac Cove and was shot during the assault on the hill known as Baby 700. The Number Eight toured twice with the Lions and stayed on in Australia following the 1904 trip, later winning a cap for the Wallabies.

## THURSDAY 25th APRIL 1974

1966 Lion David Watkins scored the last of his 929 Salford RLFC points in a record run of scoring in 92 consecutive games for one club. During his scoring streak Watkins scored 41 tries and 403 goals for the Red Devils. The fly-half toured Australia and New Zealand with Mike Campbell-Lamerton's Lions. Watkins scored 43 points over 21 matches on the Tour. He played in all five Tests and took over the captaincy for two matches against the All Blacks after Campbell-Lamerton dropped himself from the side.

## SATURDAY 25th APRIL 1987

1983 tourist and Ulster captain David Irwin was caught in an IRA bomb blast while travelling with two teammates from Belfast to Dublin for training with Ireland. The bomb exploded near the Irish border killing Lord Justice Maurice Gibson and his wife. Irwin emerged relatively unscathed but the incident ended the career of flanker Nigel Carr while full-back Philip Rainey suffered a head injury that prevented him from playing in the inaugural Rugby World Cup. Irwin said: "I was driving the car at the time and, for some reason, I managed to escape with singed hair and eyebrows. I managed to drag Nigel out, after some trouble shifting him, and went back for Philip."

## SATURDAY 26th APRIL 1975

Budge Rogers captained Bedford to a 28-12 win over Rosslyn Park in the RFU's Knock-Out Cup in front of 18,000 at Twickenham. The veteran flanker had earned 34 English caps between 1961 and 1969 as well as touring South Africa with the 1962 Lions. Rogers played 12 times on Tour and won two Test caps.

## TUESDAY 27th APRIL 1965

William Oldham died in Poole, England aged 77. The England forward toured New Zealand and Australia with Arthur 'Boxer' Harding's side in 1908. He played in the first Test against New Zealand but after the Lions suffered a heavy 32-5 defeat in Dunedin he was not selected for any further international matches. In all Oldham played 13 matches for the Lions scoring one try against Manawatu.

## SATURDAY 28th APRIL 1888

The British & Irish Lions beat Otago in their first ever match, which was played at the Caledonian Ground in Dunedin in front of 10,000 spectators. Despite Tom Kent's try the tourists trailed 3–1 at halftime and they were expected to flag in the second half following their long sea voyage. Instead they rallied to play "harder and rougher", combining well to score two dropped goals through Harry Speakman and another try, this time for Jack Anderton, to win the match 8-3.

## WEDNESDAY 28th APRIL 1948

Wales and Lions centre Bleddyn Williams scored four tries for Cardiff as Gloucester were thrashed 33-3 at the Arms Park. The scores took Williams' total for the season to 41 tries, a figure that remains the club record for a single campaign. Also on the scoresheet against Gloucester with a try was Jack Matthews who formed a famous midfield partnership with Williams for club, country and the Lions. The pair toured New Zealand and Australia together in 1950 and played five Tests paired at centre.

## FRIDAY 29th APRIL 1955

1938 Lion Bill Clement was awarded the Territorial Efficiency Decoration in recognition for his long service in the Territorial Army. The Llanelli wing had remained in the Territorials after the end of World War Two. Before the war he had won six Welsh caps and scored a try against Ireland in 1938. Later that year he joined Sam Walker's Lions in South Africa, scoring four tries in six Tour matches.

## SATURDAY 29th APRIL 1995

Wing Jason Robinson was rewarded with the Lance Todd Trophy for his two stunning solo tries in Wigan's 30-10 win in the Challenge Cup Final at Wembley Stadium. It was Wigan's eighth successive victory in the competition. Robinson toured twice with the Lions, in 2001 and 2005 and amongst his teammates at Wembley were Shaun Edwards and Andy Farrell who both went on to coach the Lions.

## SUNDAY 30th APRIL 1882

John Raphael was born in Brussels, Belgium. Born into a banking dynasty Raphael was educated in England at the Merchant Taylors School near London. He excelled at sports, playing for Oxford University and Surrey at cricket. He was capped by England at full-back and in 1910 led the first of the 'Lost Lions' Tours to Argentina. The Tour was a success with all six matches won, including a 28-3 victory over Argentina when Raphael was one of the try scorers. During World War One Raphael served with the King's Royal Rifle Corps as a Lieutenant, he died as a result of his wounds at the Battle of Messines.

## THURSDAY 30th APRIL 1936

Whilst returning to Britain from Rio de Janeiro on the Royal Mail ship *Arlanza* the 1910 tourist Stanley Williams fell overboard and was declared lost at sea. The full-back was still uncapped when he was selected to join captain Tommy Smyth's Lions in South Africa. The pair were part of a record contingent of seven Newport players that went on the trip. Threequarters Mel Baker, Reg Plummer and Jack Jones along with forwards Harry Jarman and Phil Waller all represented the Rodney Parade club on the trip – a record that stood until 2005 when eight Leicester Tigers players joined Clive Woodward's mammoth 51-man squad in New Zealand.

## SATURDAY 30th APRIL 1960

British & Irish Lions Arthur Smith, Gordon Waddell, Hugh McLeod and David Rollo were all in the Scotland team that lost 18-10 to South Africa in Port Elizabeth. The trip marked the first time one of the Home Nations had mounted an overseas Tour on its own.

# THE BRITISH & IRISH LIONS
## *On This Day*

# MAY

## FRIDAY 1st MAY 1874

Louis Magee was born in Dublin, Ireland. The half back was part of a sporting family and both he and his brother Joseph earned Ireland caps at rugby union. A third brother James represented Ireland at cricket and although he was never capped at rugby by his country he joined Johnny Hammond for the Lions' 1896 Tour of South Africa. Louis was also on that Tour and the brothers were part of a large Irish contingent that included Tom Crean, Robert Johnston and Larry Bulger. Magee played in all four Tests, 10 further Tour matches and scored two tries in the 16-0 win over Griqualand West.

## SUNDAY 2nd MAY 1982

Limerick United won the FAI Cup for the second time in the club's history seeing off Dublin side Bohemians 1-0 at Dalymount Park. Brendan Storan scored the winner in the 34th minute slamming home the ball from Tony Ward's low corner. As well as playing football Ward was a rugby union international who played fly-half for Ireland and toured South Africa with Bill Beaumont's Lions team. Ward played in five matches and scored 48 points on the 1980 Tour. In the opening Test he kicked five penalties and a dropped goal to set the individual Lions points record of 18 points versus South Africa that stood for 29 years.

## TUESDAY 3rd MAY 1955

Colin Deans was born in Hawick, Scotland. The hooker made his name with his hometown club before making his Scotland debut in 1978. As well as being a technically sound hooker and accurate lineout thrower Deans was a fast, dynamic player in the loose and often acted as an extra flanker. The highlight of his Scotland career was the 1984 Grand Slam and he earned 52 Scottish caps, a record at the time. He toured New Zealand with the 1983 Lions and despite excellent form was considered unfortunate not to win a Test cap. He was restricted to seven non-international appearances but was selected for the 1986 Lions match against a World XV for the IRB's centenary celebrations.

## MONDAY 4th MAY 1903

Fred Byrne's captaincy of Warwickshire County Cricket Club got off to a winning start as Surrey were beaten by 126 runs at Kennington Oval. Byrne was Warwickshire captain for five seasons but his cricket career didn't start until 1897 by which time his rugby career was at its peak. In 1898 the Moseley full-back had captained England in the Home Championship and two years earlier he had joined Johnny Hammond's Lions in South Africa. Byrne had played in all 21 matches of the Tour and became the first player to score over a century of points during a Tour of South Africa. His total of 100 came from seven tries, 30 conversions, seven dropped goals and six penalties.

## SATURDAY 4th MAY 1929

1924 Lion Roy Kinnear sealed Challenge Cup final victory for Wigan with the last try of a 13-2 win over Dewsbury. The final was the first to be played at Wembley Stadium and the first to be broadcast with live commentary on BBC Radio. Kinnear toured South Africa as a centre with the 1924 Lions playing in four Tests and six other matches, but did not score any points. He turned professional with Wigan three years later.

## FRIDAY 5th MAY 1972

Barry John shocked the rugby world by announcing his retirement from the sport at the age of 27 citing the pressure of "living in a goldfish bowl". He said, "I just wanted to play rugby and I felt that all the attention was affecting my form. I did not want to stop playing; I just felt I had to, if only to be fair to myself. The regret, which I still have, was not ending my career, but having no option. I felt I had at least a couple more years at the top, but only if I could be me and the celebrity thing was getting in the way of that." John won 25 caps for Wales and another five for the Lions over the 1968 and 1971 Tours.

## WEDNESDAY 5th MAY 1993

*Sharpe's Rifles* starring Sean Bean as soldier Richard Sharpe premiered on British television. It was first of a successful series charting a soldier's adventures during the Napoleonic Wars and was based on the novels of Bernard Cornwell. The title character Richard Sharpe was named after former England captain and 1962 Lion Richard Sharp. Cornwell said: "I wasted hours trying to find my hero's name... So I named him after Richard Sharp, the great rugby player, and of course the name stuck. I added an 'e', that was all."

## WEDNESDAY 6th MAY 1925

Angus Black was born in Dunfermline, Scotland. The scrum-half toured New Zealand with the 1950 Lions and was selected for the first two Tests of the series. The tourists secured a 9-9 draw in the first Test but All Black flanker Pat Crowley successfully targeted Black in the second match, disrupting his service and starving the potent Lions backline of possession. The Scot lost his place in the Test team but still completed 10 matches on the trip.

## SATURDAY 7th MAY 1927

1924 tourist Tom Holliday became the third man to score a hat-trick in rugby league's Challenge Cup final as he helped Oldham to beat Swinton 26-7 in front of 33,448 spectators at Central Park in Wigan. It was Oldham's third triumph in the competition. Three years earlier the full-back travelled to South Africa with Ronald Cove-Smith's team but only played one match as his Tour was ended early by injury.

## WEDNESDAY 8th MAY 1991

Alun Thomas died in Swansea, Wales aged 65. Thomas, who could play at either centre or wing, toured South Africa with the 1955 Lions. His Tour was interrupted by an injury that limited him to five matches and 15 points from the boot. Thomas returned to the country 19 years later as manager of Willie John McBride's undefeated Tour.

## MONDAY 8th MAY 2000

*This is Your Life* host Michael Aspel surprised England prop Jason Leonard at the launch of his testimonial year. Leonard said: "There were surprises all the way through – schoolteachers, old friends and family friends were there, many of whom I hadn't seen for years." Leonard toured three times with the Lions winning five of his 119 Test caps with the team. The others came in a successful 13-year England career that encompassed four Grand Slams and two World Cup finals.

## WEDNESDAY 9th MAY 1888

Rochdale Hornets scrum-half Johnny Nolan became the first player to score a hat-trick of tries for the British & Irish Lions. Nolan struck three times in the 4-0 win over Canterbury at Lancaster Park as the Shaw and Shrewsbury team made it four wins in a row at the start of the first Lions Tour. Nolan played in 20 of the 35 matches on the 1888 Tour and scored 15 tries in total including two hat-tricks.

## TUESDAY 9th MAY 1899

The 1899 Lions departed Charing Cross Station on the 11am train heading for the English Channel. They crossed the Channel and travelled overland to Marseilles where they boarded P&O's liner the RMS *Oceana*. A five-week ocean voyage took the tourists to Adelaide, via the Red Sea and a stop at Albany in Western Australia, for the only dedicated Tour of Australia during the Lions' first century of existence.

## WEDNESDAY 10th MAY 1950

Welsh wing Malcolm Thomas kicked a record six penalties in a Lions match as Marlborough/Nelson Bays were beaten 24-3 in the opening match of the 1950 Tour. Thomas and Ivor Preece added a try apiece to the tourists score. Thomas toured Australia and New Zealand twice with the Lions, in 1950 and 1959, playing 32 matches including four Tests and scoring 152 point from 13 tries, 21 conversions and 17 penalty goals.

## SUNDAY 10th MAY 1959

The 1959 tourists assembled at Eastbourne for a pre-flight training camp. Ireland hooker Ronnie Dawson was named captain in a squad that contained nine of his compatriots. The squad also contained six veterans of the 1955 trip to South Africa. Irish wing Tony O'Reilly, Scottish prop Hugh McLeod, the English pair Jeff Butterfield and Dickie Jeeps as well as the Welsh duo of Bryn Meredith and Rhys Williams were all making their second Lions Tour. Butterfield, who was a PE graduate, took charge of training in Eastbourne before the squad departed from London Airport bound for Melbourne.

## WEDNESDAY 11th MAY 1966

The 1966 Lions made it two wins in two matches as South Australia were brushed aside 38-11 at the Norwood Oval in Adelaide. Scottish full-back Stewart Wilson opened his account for the Tour with a penalty and a conversion. Wilson would end the Tour as the top scorer with 90 points, 30 of them in the Test matches.

## SATURDAY 11th MAY 1968

Bev Risman, a Lions tourist in 1959, won rugby league's Challenge Cup with Leeds at Wembley. Leeds triumphed 11-10 over Wakefield Trinity on a pitch so waterlogged the game was dubbed the 'Watersplash Final'. Risman kicked four penalties in the match but the final is usually remembered for Don Fox's last minute miss. Fox slipped and failed with a conversion in front of the posts to hand Leeds victory. Risman played in 14 matches of the 1959 Tour, including four Tests, and scored 62 points.

## WEDNESDAY 12th MAY 1971

A jet-lagged and rusty Lions side that had only had one practice session went down 15-11 to Queensland at Ballymore in Brisbane. The result prompted Queensland coach and former Wallaby international, Des Connor, to state: "These Lions are hopeless; they are undoubtedly the worst team ever to be sent to New Zealand." History was to prove Connor wrong as John Dawes' team only lost one more match on Tour and triumphed in the Test series against the All Blacks.

## SUNDAY 12th MAY 2002

A Leicester Tigers side crammed with British & Irish Lions and coached by Dean Richards sealed its fourth Premiership title in succession with a 34-16 win over London Irish at Welford Road. Richards toured twice with the Lions winning six Test caps during the 1989 and 1993 series. His Leicester side included Martin Johnson, Tim Stimpson, Austin Healey, Ben Kay, Lewis Moody, Geordan Murphy, Ollie Smith and Dorian West. Leicester would retain the Heineken Cup 13 days later with a 15-9 win over Munster in Cardiff.

## SATURDAY 13th MAY 1989

Outside centre Jeremy Guscott marked his England debut with a hat-trick of tries as Romania were blown away 58-3 in Bucharest. Within weeks of receiving his first England cap the 23-year-old had been called up to join the Lions Tour already in progress in Australia. Guscott also scored a try on his Lions Test debut, a perfectly judged chip and chase that sealed victory in the second international match and levelled the series. He toured twice more with the Lions and it was his dropped goal that clinched the series win in South Africa eight years later.

## MONDAY 14th MAY 1928

Stan Hodgson was born in Durham, England. The hooker was selected to tour South Africa with Arthur Smith's Lions in 1962. Hodgson, who won 11 England caps between 1960 and 1964, only managed one appearance for the tourists in the 38-9 win over Rhodesia in Salisbury. The match was the opening fixture of the Tour and Hodgson managed to score a try before a broken leg ended his involvement.

## SATURDAY 14th MAY 1983

England full-back Dusty Hare scored 21 points as Wanganui were brushed aside 47-15 at Spriggens Park in the opening encounter of the 1983 Tour. Hare's haul consisted of five penalties and three conversions, he would play in five more matches on the Tour finishing with a total of 88 points.

## WEDNESDAY 15th MAY 1974

Willie John McBride's team began their Tour in record-breaking fashion with the Lions' biggest ever win on South African soil, a 59-13 victory over Western Transvaal. Second row Gordon Brown scored the first try of the Tour. It was the first of eight he'd manage on the Tour putting him third on the scoring charts. The Lions ran in nine tries in all during the opening fixture at Olen Park. Tom David and Gareth Edwards got two each while John Moloney, Andy Ripley, Clive Rees and Billy Steele all touched down. However, injuries to Moloney and Llanelli centre Roy Bergiers took the shine off the win.

## WEDNESDAY 16th MAY 1888

The Lions suffered a reverse going down 1-0 to Taranaki Clubs at The Racecourse in New Plymouth. It was the team's first ever defeat with Taranaki prop Harry Good scoring the only point of the match with a try.

## THURSDAY 17th MAY 1900

The siege of Mafeking was lifted after 217 days. The Relief was led by Colonel Baden-Powell and was a pivotal moment in the Second Boer War. Taking part on the British side was Thomas Crean, a trooper in the Imperial Light Horse. Crean had stayed on in South Africa at the end of the 1896 Lions Tour. The Irish forward won nine caps for his country before earning selection on the Tour where he played in all 21 matches. Crean scored six tries including a hat-trick against Eastern Province and a score in the second Test. He also captained the Lions in two Test matches.

## MONDAY 17th MAY 1926

John Robins was born in Cardiff, Wales. The prop toured Australasia with the Lions in 1950 winning five caps against the All Blacks and Wallabies. He kicked 10 points in international matches and added another 29 in 15 further Tour matches. In 1966 Robins returned to Australia and New Zealand with the Lions after being appointed as the team's first coach. Although the Australian leg was a success the Lions were whitewashed 4-0 by the All Blacks and suffered a shock defeat to British Columbia on the way home.

## WEDNESDAY 18th MAY 1983

Auckland registered the fifth of their six victories over the Lions with a win at Eden Park. The New Zealand provincial side also drew with the 1888 side – who they played four times – giving Auckland the best record of any non-international opposition faced by the tourists. All Black second rows Andy Haden and Gary Whetton dominated the lineouts to set up a 13-12 win and inflict a defeat in just the second match of the 1983 Tour.

## THURSDAY 19th MAY 1938

The British & Irish Lions squad assembled at the Victoria Hotel in London. After two nights in the capital the team took the train from Waterloo Station to Southampton. There they were given a special send-off lunch as guests of the Union-Castle Line before boarding the company's flagship vessel the *Stirling Castle*. The tourists travelled first class on the 19-day voyage to Port Elizabeth.

## SATURDAY 20th MAY 1950

Otago shocked a full-strength Lions side by handing out the worst defeat of the Tour just a week before the first Test against the All Blacks. The hosts were dominating New Zealand rugby at the time with an efficient rucking style allied to effective use of second-phase ball. They gave the Lions a lesson in both of these evolving elements of the game, comprehensively outplaying the visiting forwards and outscoring them three tries to one in a 23-9 victory.

## SATURDAY 20th MAY 1961

Lewis Jones starred with a try as Leeds won the rugby league championship for the first time, beating Warrington 25-10 in the play-off final at Odsal Stadium in Bradford. The Welsh full-back was a late call up to the 1950 Tour of New Zealand and Australia. Two years later he turned professional with Leeds in a record £6,000 deal. A successful career in rugby league followed as he won the Challenge Cup in 1957, caps with Wales and Great Britain and became the first Leeds player to kick over 1,000 goals.

## SATURDAY 21st MAY 1910

The *Edinburgh Castle* departed Southampton for Cape Town with 24 Lions on board led by Tour Manager William Cail, assistant manager Walter Rees and captain Tom Smyth. The Tour party had already undergone nine changes since the initial squad was announced five weeks earlier. An injury-ravaged Tour would necessitate a number of further changes to personnel while in South Africa.

## TUESDAY 22nd MAY 1894

Herbert Castens captained the South Africa cricket team when they played their first ever fixture. The team toured England in 1894 and lost its first match to Lord Sheffield's XI at Sheffield Park in Uckfield. Castens had the honour of being South Africa's first captain at both cricket and rugby having led the Springboks in the first Test against the Lions three years earlier.

## TUESDAY 23rd MAY 1865

William Mitchell was born in Wield, England. The full-back was first capped by England in 1890 and travelled to South Africa with the first official Lions party the next year. Mitchell played in all 20 matches of the Tour scoring 20 points, including all the points in the 3-0 second Test victory with a dropped goal.

## SATURDAY 23rd MAY 1959

The Australian leg of the Lions Tour got off to the perfect start as the tourists ran in 12 tries in a 53-18 thrashing of Victoria in Melbourne. Fly-half Bev Risman led the rout with 19 points from two tries, five conversions and a penalty. Risman played in 14 matches on Tour, including four Tests, and scored 62 points.

## SUNDAY 23rd MAY 2004

Wasps scrum-half Rob Howley scored a dramatic late try, capitalising on Clement Poitrenaud's indecision, to snatch a 27-20 win over Toulouse in the Heineken Cup final at Twickenham. Howley was one of six British & Irish Lions in the victorious Wasps side in London. Also in the team, which was coached by Warren Gatland, were Lawrence Dallaglio, Tim Payne, Josh Lewsey, Joe Worsley and Simon Shaw.

## MONDAY 23rd MAY 2005

Jonny Wilkinson's late, late penalty salvaged a 25-25 draw for the Lions as they took on Argentina at the Millennium Stadium in Cardiff. The match was a warm-up for the Tour of New Zealand and both sides fielded weakened sides. Argentina were the better side on the night but Wilkinson's boot kept the Lions in touch and his sixth and final penalty came deep into stoppage time.

## THURSDAY 24th MAY 1888

Tour Manager Arthur Shrewsbury blamed the Lions' 4-0 defeat to Auckland on the rigours and temptations of touring. In a letter to co-manager Alfred Shaw he said: "We simply lost the match through our players not taking care of themselves, too much whisky and women." Auckland have since become a major thorn in the Lions' side with six victories and a draw against the tourists over the years.

## THURSDAY 25th MAY 1878

Bill MacLagan, captain of the 1891 Lions Tour, was out for a duck as Scotland's cricket team took on England in Edinburgh. It was MacLagan's second duck of the match as Scotland lost by seven wickets. Leading England's successful run chase with an unbeaten 34 in the second innings was Arthur Shrewsbury, co-manager of the 1888 Tour.

## THURSDAY 25th MAY 1944

Chris Ralston was born in Hendon, England. The second row played his club rugby for Richmond before earning an England call-up in 1971. Three years later he was selected to tour South Africa with Willie John McBride's squad. He played in 13 matches on the Tour including the fourth and final Test.

## SATURDAY 26th MAY 1962

England centre Mick Weston scored a try and kicked three penalties to top score for the Lions as Rhodesia were thrashed 38-9 at the Hartsfield Ground in Salisbury in the Tour opener. Weston toured twice with the Lions playing in 31 matches including six Tests and scoring 69 points.

## SUNDAY 26th MAY 1974

The first Battle of Boet Erasmus took place as Eastern Province tried to knock the undefeated Lions out of their stride with a physical assault. The home side were fired up after Springbok Head Coach Johan Claassen gave a pre-match pep talk and a violent match followed. Lions flanker Roger Uttley said: "There was fighting left, right and centre with Stewart McKinney and Mike Burton in the middle of it – the boys weren't going to be messed about." The Lions were determined not to be intimidated and won the match by a 28-14 scoreline.

## SATURDAY 27th MAY 1950

All Black centre Ron Elvidge's late try denied the British & Irish Lions victory in the first Test of the 1950 series, which finished 9-9 at Carisbrook in Dunedin. The Lions had gone into the match as underdogs after losses to Otago and Southland that had seen the forwards dominated. However, the pack put in a fine display and the Lions led 9-3 late in the second half through Jackie Kyle's and Ken Jones' tries while John Robins had added a penalty. Roy Roper's solo effort had put the hosts on the scoreboard and late on a Bob Scott penalty reduced the deficit to three points before Elvidge levelled the scores. Lions centre Bleddyn Williams said: "We were pleased to have held the All Blacks in the first Test, when our forwards showed their claws. What a pity the forwards did not play again with the same tigerish tenacity. It was as if they had burnt themselves out in that one game."

## SATURDAY 28th MAY 1966

A crowd of 42,303 watched the first Test between the Lions and the Wallabies at the Sydney Cricket Ground. The attendance was a record for an Australian rugby union match at the time and the bumper crowd saw the Lions overturn an 8-0 half-time deficit. On a good day for the Irish front row union prop Ray McLoughlin and hooker Ken Kennedy scored tries from lineout moves while full-back Don Rutherford added a conversion and a penalty to give the Lions an 11-8 victory.

## TUESDAY 29th MAY 1956

Colonel Mike Campbell-Lamerton led two platoons of the Duke of Wellington's Regiment during the Battle of Hook in the Korean War. The unit distinguished themselves during the battle, recovering several positions that had previously been overrun by a Chinese offensive. The Number Eight made his Scotland debut three years later and twice toured with the Lions. Campbell-Lamerton played 20 times on the 1962 trip to South Africa winning four Test caps and scoring three tries. He led the party to Australasia four years later winning another four caps.

## WEDNESDAY 29th MAY 1974

The Lions roared to their biggest ever victory on South African soil with a 97-0 mauling of South Western Districts at the Van Riebeeck Ground in Mossel Bay. Welsh wing JJ Williams scored a record-equalling six tries in the match while English fly-half Alan Old set the Lions point scoring record with 37. Old's tally of 15 conversions remains unmatched and he added a try and a penalty for good measure. The Lions ran in 16 tries in all with Geoff Evans getting a hat-trick while JPR Williams scored two. Fergus Slattery, Mervyn Davies, John Moloney and Tom Grace all touched down during the rout.

## SATURDAY 29th MAY 1993

England prop Jason Leonard inspired the Lions to a late comeback against the New Zealand Maori at Athletic Park in Wellington. The Lions were trailing 20-3 with just 15 minutes left to play when Leonard came on to rally the pack. Late tries from Ieuan Evans, Rory Underwood and Gavin Hastings, which were all converted by the latter, gave the Lions a 24-20 victory to preserve the unbeaten start to the Tour.

## SATURDAY 30th MAY 1908

Otago made it two defeats for the Lions in the opening three matches of the 1908 Tour with a 9-6 win at Carisbrook in Dunedin. It was Otago's first victory over the Lions, although they had managed a draw against the 1888 team, and was the first of their five victories over the tourists, the most recent coming in 1993.

## SATURDAY 30th MAY 2009

The 2009 Tour got off to an inauspicious start as Paul O'Connell's side struggled to beat the Royal XV in the opening fixture. The Lions trailed 25-13 with only 10 minutes left to play when Welsh full-back Lee Byrne's solo effort sparked a late comeback. Converted tries from Alun Wyn-Jones and Ronan O'Gara followed as the Lions came back to win 37-25.

## THURSDAY 31st MAY 1951

Arthur O'Brien died in Christchurch, New Zealand aged 73. The New Zealander came to England to study medicine at Guy's Hospital in London. O'Brien, who played at centre, was one of four Guy's players to be selected to tour Australia and New Zealand. The others were O'Brien's fellow Kiwi Pat McEvedy and forwards David Trail and Stuart Saunders. O'Brien was elected to act as Tour Manager and played in 16 of the 19 matches on the trip. He scored a try in the second Test against Australia and kicked 15 conversions on the Tour.

## SATURDAY 31st MAY 1980

The Springboks outscored the Lions five tries to one in the first Test at Newlands. Willie de Plessis, Gerrie Germishuys, Divan Serfontein, Rob Louw, Moaner van Heerden all scored tries for South Africa while Welsh prop Graham Price got the Lions' solitary reply. The boot of Tony Ward kept the tourists in touch as he racked up 18 points with five penalties and a dropped goal. It was not enough though and the hosts ran out 26-22 victors.

# THE BRITISH & IRISH LIONS
## *On This Day*

SINCE 1888

# JUNE

## THURSDAY 1st JUNE 1916

The Battle of Jutland concluded near the coast of Denmark in the North Sea. The battle was the major naval engagement of World War One with the British Grand Fleet and German High Seas Fleet engaging twice before withdrawing. Despite heavy loss of life and ships the result of the battle was inconclusive. Aboard HMS *Warspite* serving as chaplain was Walter Carey who played as a forward for Oxford University, Blackheath and the Barbarians. Despite never being capped for England Carey toured South Africa in 1896 with Jonny Hammond's Lions team. Carey played in all four Test matches scoring a try in the opener at Port Elizabeth.

## WEDNESDAY 1st JUNE 1977

Wanganui were thrashed 60-9 with Scotland full-back Andy Irvine running in five tries. Irvine toured three times with the Lions making 42 appearances, including winning nine Test caps. He is the team's record points scorer with 274. Irvine finished the 1977 Tour with 87 points from 11 tries, eight conversions and nine penalties.

## SATURDAY 1st JUNE 2013

The Lions swept the Barbarians aside 59-8 in the Tour opener at the Hong Kong Stadium – the team's first visit to China. The tourists scored eight tries with Ireland's Paul O'Connell opening the scoring for the Lions before the Welsh contingent added the rest. Jonathan Davies, Dan Lydiate and Alun Wyn Jones got a try apiece while Mike Phillips and Alex Cuthbert touched down twice each. England fly-half Owen Farrell kicked 18 points while Jonathan Sexton added another six. Samoan scrum-half Kahn Fotuali'i scored the Baa-Baas' solitary try while 21-year-old English centre Elliot Daly kicked a penalty.

## SATURDAY 2nd JUNE 1888

The Governor of New South Wales, Lord Carrington, was amongst the 18,000 crowd at the Association Cricket Ground in Sydney that saw the Lions' first ever match on Australian soil. The Lions beat New South Wales 18-2 with Salford forward Harry Eagles scoring both the first points and first try for the Lions in Australia.

## TUESDAY 2nd JUNE 1959

Ireland wing Tony O'Reilly took up where he had left off from the previous Tour with two tries on his first appearance in 1959 as Queensland were comfortably beaten 39-11 at the Exhibition Grounds in Brisbane. O'Reilly had scored a record 22 tries on the 1955 trip to South Africa and would add another 16 on the Tour of New Zealand and Australia. His total of 38 tries in all matches remains a Lions record as does his tally of six Test tries.

## FRIDAY 3rd JUNE 1938

The Union Castle-Line's flagship vessel, the *Stirling Castle*, arrived in Cape Town with Sam Walker's touring party on board. The Lions' two-week voyage had begun in Southampton and taken in a stop in Madeira. After a welcome luncheon at Cape Town City Hall and a training session at Green Point Track the Lions re-embarked on the *Stirling Castle* and sailed to East London for their first fixture against Border.

## WEDNESDAY 4th JUNE 1930

The day after losing 12-8 to Wellington the touring party relaxed by either playing a round at the Heretaunga golf links or touring the waterfront of New Zealand's capital city. In the afternoon the Lions party was entertained at the home of Dr Pat McEvedy, who had toured with the 1904 and 1908 Lions whilst a medical student in London, before returning to his native New Zealand to set up practice.

## SATURDAY 4th JUNE 1966

The Lions romped to a Test record 31-0 victory as Australia were overwhelmed at Lang Park in Brisbane. London Scottish and Scotland full-back Stewart Wilson's penalty gave the tourists a 3-0 half-time lead, which was doubled when David Watkins dropped a goal shortly after the restart. The Lions ran riot in the final quarter scoring 25 points in the final 22 minutes. Welsh wing Ken Jones scored two tries with Dewi Bebb, Noel Murphy and Watkins adding one apiece. Wilson converted all five Lions tries to finish with a personal haul of 13 in what remains the biggest winning margin achieved by the Lions in a Test.

## TUESDAY 4th JUNE 1974

The Lions broke new ground when the South African government sanctioned a match against the SAR Federation XV, a team made up of players deemed 'coloured' under apartheid. The controversial fixture was won comfortably 37-6 but the victory came at a high price for Alan Old whose leg was badly damaged by a late tackle that ended his Tour.

## SATURDAY 4th JUNE 1983

The Lions lost the first Test 16-12 on a greasy surface at Lancaster Park in Christchurch. The difference between the sides was an unconverted try scored by All Blacks flanker Mark Shaw after the two kickers had cancelled each other out. New Zealand full-back Allan Hewson and Lions fly-half Ollie Campbell each kicked three penalties and a dropped goal.

## FRIDAY 5th JUNE 1891

The RFU's announcement in *The Times* revealed the 21-man squad for the Lions' first ever Tour of South Africa. Scotland's Bill MacLagan was persuaded out of international retirement to captain the side at the age of 33. His party included nine internationals and 12 uncapped players and was managed by the RFU's Edwin Ash. The team was entirely made up of Scots and English. Scotland had claimed the title in that year's home championship and their two leading try scorers, Paul Clauss and William Wotherspoon, both travelled along with forward Robert MacMillan.

## SATURDAY 6th JUNE 1908

The Lions suffered a heavy defeat in their second ever Test on New Zealand soil and first at Carisbrook in Dunedin. Defeats to Wellington and Otago in the build-up to the first Test had been less than ideal preparation and the All Blacks exposed weaknesses in the tourists' backline to run in seven tries in a 32-5 victory.

## SATURDAY 6th JUNE 1959

Ireland wing Tony O'Reilly and Scotland flanker Ken Smith scored tries as the Lions ran out easy 17-6 winners in the first Test in Brisbane. Bev Risman kicked a conversion, David Hewitt added two penalties and Ken Scotland slotted over a dropped goal as the Lions went one up in the series.

## SATURDAY 7th JUNE 1997

A week before the first Test the Lions were dominated in the scrum by Northern Transvaal who inflicted the first defeat of the Tour and the first by a South African province for 29 years. The final score of 35-30 would have been far less flattering for the Lions but for three tries conjured against the run of play by the combined magic of Gregor Townsend and Jeremy Guscott.

## FRIDAY 8th JUNE 1888

The day after beating Bathurst 13-6 the Lions went out kangaroo hunting in the mountains of New South Wales. In a letter to the Manchester Courier captain Robert Seddon wrote: "The scenery here was simply wonderful. I was so lost in my admiration that I had almost forgotten the shooting and rambled down the rocks, but was brought up short by hearing a gun shot and feeling a few pellets down my back. In a very short time I had forgotten the scenery and rushed for safety. The day's outing was one of the most enjoyable we have had. Getting the spoil together we found that our day's sport resulted in bagging about 120 kangaroos and hares."

## SATURDAY 8th JUNE 1974

Willie John McBride's side came out on top in an attritional first Test in Cape Town. The Lions triumphed 12-3 after dominating the Springboks in the host's traditional area of strength in the scrum. Fly-half Phil Bennett kicked three penalties while his half back partner Gareth Edwards added a dropped goal.

## FRIDAY 8th JUNE 2001

Records tumbled at the WACA in Perth as the Lions thrashed Western Australia by a record score of 116-10. The Lions ran in a record 18 tries against hopelessly outmatched, and largely amateur, opposition with Welsh Number Eight Scott Quinnell and English wing Dan Luger claiming a hat-trick apiece. The points tally of 116 remains the highest achieved by a Lions team in any match and the winning margin of 106 is a record too. Irish fly-half Ronan O'Gara converted 13 of the tries for 26 points, both figures are records for the Lions in Australian matches.

## WEDNESDAY 8th JUNE 2005

The Lions 36-14 victory over Taranaki was marred by an incident in which touch judge Steve Walsh verbally abused Ireland wing Shane Horgan. Walsh was later suspended from officiating for four months.

## THURSDAY 9th JUNE 1938

Ulster forward Norman Brand died in Poole, Dorset aged 39. The 1924 tourist drowned in an accident in the town's harbour. Brand was selected to Tour with Ronald Cove-Smith's side, although uncapped at the time, and played in four provincial matches and the first two Tests of the series. Brand won his solitary Ireland cap later that year in a 6-0 defeat against New Zealand at Lansdowne Road.

## SATURDAY 10th JUNE 1950

All the points came in the first half as New Zealand took the lead in the 1950 series with an 8-0 win at Lancaster Park in Christchurch. All Black flanker Pat Crowley opened the scoring with a try before the Lions went down to 14 men as his opposite number Bill McKay left the field with a broken nose. Centre Roy Roper doubled the home side's lead with a try that fly-half Laurie Haig converted.

## WEDNESDAY 11th JUNE 1997

English wing John Bentley scored one of the most memorable tries in Lions history with a 60-metre dash that took him past five defenders as the Gauteng Lions were overcome 20-14. It was also a key moment of the 1997 Tour with the squad depleted by injuries and suspensions while morale had been dented by a 35-30 defeat to Northern Transvaal. The Lions trailed 9-3 at the break before Austin Healey sidestepped his way over for their first try at Ellis Park. The brilliance of Bentley and kicking accuracy of Neil Jenkins sealed the win. Bentley said: "We play a sport that lends itself to individuals having special moments. There is no doubt that that was a very special moment for me and it continues to be talked about today."

JOHN BENTLEY ON HIS WAY TO THE LINE

## TUESDAY 12th JUNE 1888

The British & Irish Lions were held to a 10-10 draw by King's School, Parramatta, in what was described as the toughest match that Robert Seddon's side faced on the Australian leg of the 1888 Tour. The Lions trailed a Past and Present XV that included Charles Gregory Wade, the former England wing who would go on to become Premier of New South Wales. With only five minutes left to play the Lions were behind 10-8 before Jack Anderton's second try of the match levelled the scores.

## SUNDAY 12th JUNE 1910

The Lions provided the opposition at the Polo Ground of Flores in Buenos Aires as Argentina played their first ever Test match. The Lions outclassed the Pumas, who were largely made up of expatriates and included former Springbok Fairie Heatlie at Number Eight, winning 28-3. Wing Harold Monks score two tries for the Lions as well as kicking a dropped goal. Captain John Raphael touched down and kicked a conversion while forwards William Fraser and Horace Ward also scored tries.

## FRIDAY 12th JUNE 2015

Wales and Lions scrum-half Sir Gareth Edwards was knighted in the Queen's Birthday Honours. Edwards is widely acknowledged as one of the greatest rugby players of all time. He won 53 caps for Wales and was part of three Grand Slam winning sides. He first toured with the Lions in 1968 and was one of the few successes of a poor Tour. Edwards' half back partnership with Barry John was vital to both Welsh success and the Lions' 1971 triumph in New Zealand. He was the key player three years later as the Lions beat the Springboks in South Africa.

## SATURDAY 13th JUNE 1959

The five tries the Lions ran in at the Sports Ground in Sydney remains a record in a Test versus Australia. The Lions were convincing 24-3 winners over the Wallabies as they took the series 2-0. Welsh centre Malcolm Price touched down twice with wings Tony O'Reilly and Bev Risman getting one apiece and captain Ronnie Dawson also crossing the whitewash.

## TUESDAY 14th JUNE 1977

The British & Irish Lions' 39-match unbeaten run came to an abrupt end as they suffered a shock 21-9 defeat to NZ Universities at Lancaster Park in Christchurch. The tourists had not lost a match since the second Test of the 1971 series at the same venue.

## SATURDAY 14th JUNE 1980

A Lions performance riddled with errors helped South Africa take an unbeatable 2-0 lead in the Test series. Springbok full-back Gysie Pienaar punished a poor Lions kicking display repeatedly launching damaging counter-attacks. South Africa scored four tries though Rob Louw, Thinus Stofberg, Gerrie Germishuys and Pienaar while Naas Botha kicked 10 points. Ireland flanker John O'Driscoll and Wales centre Ray Gravell touched down for the Lions while Andy Irvine kicked a huge penalty. Wales fly-half Gareth Davies kicked eight points but suffered a knee injury that ended his Tour.

## WEDNESDAY 15th JUNE 2005

Despite an error-strewn performance in sodden conditions the midweek side kept its 100% record intact with a 23-6 victory against Wellington. Welshmen Gethin Jenkins and Gareth Thomas scored tries while Jonny Wilkinson kicked two conversions and three penalties. Among the replacements used by Wellington was Riki Flutey, who would go on to win caps for England and tour South Africa with the Lions four years later becoming one of only two men, the other is Irish lock Tom Reid, to have played for and against the Lions in Tour matches.

## WEDNESDAY 16th JUNE 1971

An astonishing first half performance saw England wing David Duckham score five tries as West-Coast Buller were brushed aside 39-6 in Greymouth. Duckham added another score in the second half to set the individual Lions record for any match with six. The haul helped Duckham to a total of 11 tries in 17 matches on the Tour of Australasia. The Coventry-born wing was famous for his array of swerves and sidesteps and his ability to wrong foot opponents. He won 36 caps for England, scoring six tries, and played in another three Tests for the Lions against New Zealand.

## WEDNESDAY 17th JUNE 1891

Union-Castle Line shipping magnate Sir Donald Currie entertained the Lions on board the *Dunottar Castle* in the East India Docks in London. The touring party sailed for Southampton the following day before setting sail for South Africa via Madeira.

## SATURDAY 17th JUNE 1950

Welsh full-back Lewis Jones boarded the BOAC Stratocruiser aircraft Speedbird at London Airport as he headed out to join the British & Irish Lions in New Zealand. Jones had been called up as a replacement for Irish full-back George Norton who had been injured during the 8-0 loss to the All Black in the second Test a week earlier. Jones was the first Lion ever to fly out to a Tour arriving at Whenupai airport in Auckland after a two-day air trip with stops in Shannon in Ireland, Gander in Canada, New York and Honolulu in the USA. Jones would make a significant impact on the Tour playing 12 times and scoring 112 points.

## SATURDAY 18th JUNE 1977

New Zealand wing Grant Batty's interception try clinched a narrow win for the hosts in the first Test at Athletic Park in Wellington. Shortly before half-time the Lions were leading 12-10 and building a promising attack when Batty struck. It was the wing's 45th and final All Blacks try as a leg injury forced his retirement after this match. The score made it 16-12 at the break and neither side could add to their points in the second half.

## SATURDAY 18th JUNE 1983

The 1983 tourists missed a golden opportunity to level the series at a windswept Athletic Park in Wellington. Playing into a fierce first-half wind the Lions managed to restrict the All Blacks to nine points. New Zealand scrum-half Dave Loveridge opened the scoring with a try that was converted by full-back Allan Hewson, who also added a penalty. The Lions turned round optimistic that they could take advantage of conditions but were foiled by a superbly disciplined All Black pack that was brilliantly marshalled by Loveridge and the match finished 9-0.

## THURSDAY 19th JUNE 1919

1910 tourist Edward Crean was elected to the Royal Aero Club of the UK. The forward toured South Africa with Tommy Smyth's Lions playing in four matches. Following the outbreak of World War One he joined the Royal Flying Corps and rose to the rank of captain.

## SATURDAY 19th JUNE 1971

Scotland prop Sandy Carmichael suffered a broken jaw as the 1971 tour descended into violence at Lancaster Park in Christchurch. Fergus Slattery had two teeth loosened by an Alex Wyllie punch while John Pullin was hit from behind with a rabbit punch. Carmichael played on until the final whistle despite his injuries and the visitors won 14-3 on the pitch, while the local press commented: "New Zealand rugby has become as grotesque as a wounded bull."

## SATURDAY 20th JUNE 1959

The Lions began the New Zealand leg of their Tour with an emphatic 52-12 win over Hawke's Bay in Napier. Ken Scotland marked his first appearance on New Zealand soil with a hat-trick. The full-back scored 12 tries in all on the Tour and added another 36 points with his boot in 22 appearances that included five Tests.

## SATURDAY 20th JUNE 2009

A stirring second-half comeback fell just short as South Africa held on to win the first test 26-21 at the ABSA Stadium in Durban. The home side had started much the stronger with Springbok skipper John Smit crashing over for the first try after just five minutes. The Lions struggled to get to grips with the opposition or referee Bryce Lawrence's interpretation of the scrum and ruck laws. Tom Croft's try gave them hope but the Springboks extended their lead early in the second half through a converted Heinrich Brussow score before the Lions fightback began. Croft added a second try and scrum-half Mike Phillips also touched down but the Lions ultimately ran out of time.

## SATURDAY 21st JUNE 1930

The Lions won a Test against the All Blacks for the first time with a 6-3 victory at Carisbrook in Dunedin. Harlequins and England wing Jim Reeves took Roger Spong's cross kick to score the only points of the first half. The home side struck back after the break with wing George Hart finishing off a backline move for an unconverted try that levelled the scores. New Zealand were pressing for a score late in the game when Ivor Jones intercepted a pass before sending Jack Morley away for the match-winning try.

## SATURDAY 21st JUNE 1997

Late tries from scrum-half Matt Dawson and wing Alan Tait sealed a 25-16 win against the odds in the first Test at Newlands. The Lions had come into the match as underdogs against the reigning world champions. However, the decision to field a short front row of Scotland's Tom Smith along with Irishmen Paul Wallace and Keith Wood proved a masterstroke that neutralised the larger, more powerful Springbok scrum. The home side led through tries for giant prop Os Du Randt and wing Russell Bennett while the boot of Neil Jenkins kept the Lions in touch. After 69 minutes Bennett had a second try ruled out for a forward pass before Dawson produced an outrageous dummy from a scrum that allowed him to go over unopposed. Tait capped victory in the final minute touching down after an impressive move that featured most of the Lions side.

## SATURDAY 22nd JUNE 1968

Lions captain Tom Kiernan kicked two penalties as the tourists held South Africa to a 6-6 draw in Port Elizabeth.

## SATURDAY 22nd JUNE 1974

Welsh fly-half Phil Bennett's virtuoso performance helped the Lions inflict the biggest defeat in Springbok history in the second Test. South Africa flanker Morne du Plessis said: "I remember that Phil Bennett was sensational that day. But you also had JPR, JJ, Gareth – they ran rings around us frankly." The Lions ran out 28-9 winners at Loftus Versfeld in Pretoria. JJ Williams scored two tries with Bennett, Gordon Brown and Dick Milliken also touching down.

MATT DAWSON DIRECTS THE PACK

## SATURDAY 22nd JUNE 2013

A slip from Australian full-back Kurtley Beale meant that the Lions maintained their unbeaten run in Brisbane Tests with a 23-21 win. Beale had a chance to win the match with the last kick but lost his footing and his penalty narrowly missed the target. Australia had taken the lead when scrum-half Will Genia weaved his magic from a quick tap penalty and Israel Folau collected his chip to sprint over. George North hit back for the Lions with a spectacular solo effort that was matched by Folau with his second try. In the second half a makeshift Wallaby midfield was sliced wide open by Welsh wing Alex Cuthbert who touched down under the posts. Halfpenny added both conversions for the Lions as he kicked 13 vital points whereas the Australian kickers, James O'Connor and Beale, missed five attempts between them.

## SATURDAY 23rd JUNE 1894

Larry Bulger, one of the 1896 tourists, was amongst the delegates at the Sorbonne who voted unanimously to revive the Olympic Games at the inaugural Olympic Congress in Paris. Bulger was an Irish sprint champion and had been invited to the Congress through his links to athletics. Playing on the wing he would go on to win eight caps for Ireland and another four for the Lions, for whom he scored one international try. Overall he scored 19 tries in 20 matches on the Tour of South Africa.

## SUNDAY 23rd JUNE 1996

1993 Lions captain Gavin Hastings kicked an extra point from the first touchdown of the match as the Scottish Claymores won the World Bowl with a 32-27 victory over Frankfurt Galaxy at Murrayfield.

## SATURDAY 23rd JUNE 2001

The Lions 41-24 win over the New South Wales Waratahs at the Sydney Football Stadium was marred by an unprovoked assault on Ronan O'Gara. Waratah's fly-half Duncan McRae rained in 11 punches to O'Gara's face while he was pinned, defenceless, to the ground. O'Gara required eight stitches in a facial injury following the incident while McRae was sent off and later received a seven-week suspension.

## SATURDAY 24th JUNE 1899

Gwyn Nicholls became the first Welshman to win a Test cap for the British & Irish Lions as the side played their first ever Test match against Australia. The match at the Sydney Cricket Ground was also the Wallabies' first ever Test against any opposition. The Lions were still struggling to regain fitness after their five-week boat trip to Australia and were made to pay as the Wallabies scored three tries to triumph 13-3. Nicholls finished a seven-man handling move to give the Lions parity early in the second half but it was the hosts who finished stronger with two converted tries.

## TUESDAY 24th JUNE 1997

The Lions' 52-30 win over Orange Free State in Bloemfontein was overshadowed by centre Will Greenwood's near death experience following a tackle. Greenwood, who was wearing Number 12 rather than his usual lucky 13, had Lions doctor James Robson to thank for saving his life as he incurred a head injury that left him unconscious. He said: "I had swallowed my tongue, my pupils were not reacting to light, my throat was about to be cut open to free up the airways. I can tell you that there was no out-of-body experience, no going towards the light. I just was not going to wake up. Then it happened. With Robbo's help and my mum's howls I came to." Greenwood, who was the last player to receive a Lions call-up whilst still uncapped, played six matches and scored one try before his Tour was ended by this injury.

## SATURDAY 25th JUNE 1955

The Lions made it two wins from two in South Africa with a 24-14 victory over Griqualand West at the De Beers Stadium in Kimberley. Despite being picked for both matches Welsh forward Clem Thomas had to withdraw twice due to ill health. Griqualand's president Norman Weinberg, who was a prominent South African surgeon, diagnosed appendicitis and performed the operation himself. Thomas recovered in time to play in the final two Tests of the drawn series as well as eight other Tour matches.

## SATURDAY 25th JUNE 2005

Irish centre Brian O'Driscoll's Test captaincy lasted less than two minutes as he was the victim of a spear tackle from All Blacks Tana Umaga and Keven Mealamu that dislocated his shoulder. The incident marked that start of a disastrous Test for the Lions who were outplayed in all areas. Flanker Richard Hill limped off less than 20 minutes in and second row Paul O'Connell was yellow carded as the tourists' lineout disintegrated. Ali Williams and Sitiveni Sivivatu scored tries and Dan Carter kicked 11 points as New Zealand eased to a 21-3 win that might have been even more emphatic if not for the atrocious weather conditions.

## MONDAY 26th JUNE 1967

Nine candidates arrived at the East India Club in Russell Square, London to be interviewed for the posts of Tour Manager and assistant manager for the following year's series in South Africa. England's David Brooks was appointed as Tour Manager with 1959 Lions captain Ronnie Dawson taking the role of assistant.

## SATURDAY 26th JUNE 1971

Scotland prop Ian McLauchlan scored his one and only Lions try to set the tourists on course for a 9-3 win in the first Test at Carisbrook, Dunedin. McLauchlan charged down an Alan Sutherland clearance kick and ran it in for the opening points of the series. New Zealand full-back Fergie McCormack levelled the scores with a penalty but two successful Barry John kicks clinched victory for the Lions.

## SATURDAY 26th JUNE 1993

The Lions recorded their biggest Test victory in New Zealand to level the series at 1-1. The tourists ran out 20-7 winners in Wellington thanks to a superb second-half display. Having led 9-7 at the break thanks to two Gavin Hastings penalties and a Rob Andrew dropped goal the Lions kept the All Blacks scoreless in the second period. Hastings added two more penalties and left wing Rory Underwood raced 50 metres for a try after scrum-half Dewi Morris had started a counter-attack that saw Jeremy Guscott draw New Zealand full-back John Kirwan before putting the wing away for the score.

## SATURDAY 27th JUNE 2009

The Lions suffered heartbreak as the second Test and the series were lost with the last kick of the match. Springbok replacement fly-half Morne Steyn kicked a last gasp penalty from inside his own half to snatch victory for the home side, after Ronan O'Gara had ill-advisedly tried to force a result rather than kicking the ball dead and settling for a draw. Chasing his own kick ahead O'Gara took out Fourie de Preez in the air and was duly punished by Steyn. It was a dramatic end to a pulsating, and extremely physical, contest. Rob Kearney opened the scoring for the Lions with a try before Stephen Jones kicked a record-equalling 20 points. However, tries from JP Pietersen, Bryan Habana and Jaque Fourie set up the victory for the Springboks.

## SATURDAY 28th JUNE 1997

The Lions became only the third side in the 20th century to clinch a series victory on South African soil after a tremendous rearguard action in Durban. The wounded Springboks reacted ferociously to defeat the previous week launching an onslaught at the Lions. Despite heroic defending the visitors could not prevent Joost van der Westhuizen, Andre Joubert and debutant Percy Montgomery touching down. Crucially the Springboks missed all three conversions as well as three penalties. On the other hand Lions full-back Neil Jenkins was metronomic and his five penalties kept the scores level. Then late in the match the Lions marched downfield to set up centre Jeremy Guscott's dropped goal that sealed an 18-15 win.

## SATURDAY 29th JUNE 1968

Cardiff and Wales prop John O'Shea became the first British & Irish Lion to be sent off in 64 years, and the first ever to be dismissed for violent conduct, as Eastern Transvaal were overcome 37-9 in the 'Battle of the Springs.' O'Shea sought retribution after scrum-half Roger Young was struck by one of the home team. Despite being outnumbered in the ensuing melee referee Bert Woolley singled out O'Shea and sent him from the field. O'Shea said: "After my departure from the field the management sent a message to the dressing room: 'Get dressed as quickly as you can and take your place in the grandstand... And hold your head up.'"

## TUESDAY 29th JUNE 1993

The midweek side fell to its fourth and final defeat of the Tour with a surprisingly heavy 38-10 loss to Waikato. The hosts ran in five tries including one scored by hooker, and future Lions coach, Warren Gatland.

## SATURDAY 29th JUNE 2013

Welsh full-back Leigh Halfpenny kicked five penalties in a tight, attritional Test match in Melbourne. However, Australian centre Adam Ashley-Cooper scored the only try of the match in the 74th minute and his midfield partner Christian Lealiifano kicked a vital conversion to add to his three first-half penalties. Halfpenny had a chance to win the match in the final minute but his long-range penalty attempt fell agonisingly just short of the crossbar.

## WEDNESDAY 30th JUNE 1948

Walter Rees stood down as secretary of the Welsh Rugby union after 52 years service in the role. Rees had been appointed as secretary of Neath RFC in 1888 and joined the WRU a year later. He famously undertook a scouting mission to Gloucester to see the Original All Blacks play in 1905 and his analysis helped Wales inflict the only defeat on those tourists. Five years later Rees managed the Lions team that toured South Africa where a hard fought series ended in a 2-1 victory for the Springboks.

## SATURDAY 30th JUNE 2001

Stunning tries from Jason Robinson and Brian O'Driscoll were the highlights of the Lions' first Test demolition of Australia at the Gabba in Brisbane. Robinson scored the first try leaving Australian full-back Chris Latham clutching at thin air as he sped through the narrowest of gaps on the short side. The English wing then made a break that was finished by Dafydd James for a second before the break. O'Driscoll waltzed through the Wallaby defence for a third before Scott Quinnell rumbled over. The Australians scored two late tries when the Lions were down to 14 men to make the final score 29-13.

# THE BRITISH & IRISH LIONS
## *On This Day*

# JULY

## SATURDAY 1st JULY 1950

New Zealand took an unassailable 2-0 lead in the Test series with a narrow 6-3 win over the Lions at Athletic Park in Wellington. The tourists had led at half-time thanks to prop John Robins' penalty. Despite being reduced to six forwards by injuries the All Black pack dominated their Lions counterparts in the second half to give their backs a platform for victory. New Zealand centre Ron Elvidge scored the only try of the match before full-back Bob Scott kicked the match-winning penalty.

## SATURDAY 1st JULY 1989

An unbeaten Lions side went down to a shock defeat in the first Test at the Sydney Football Stadium. The Wallabies pack dominated proceedings and gave half backs Nick Farr-Jones and Michael Lynagh the platform to set up a convincing 30-12 victory. Lloyd Walker, Scott Gourlay, Dominic Maguire and Greg Martin scored tries while Lynagh kicked 14 points. For the Lions Scots Gavin Hastings and Craig Chalmers kicked six points each as the tourists were forced into a major rethink for the second Test.

## SATURDAY 2nd JULY 1904

After a scoreless first half the Lions scored 17 unanswered points to win the first Test at the Sydney Cricket Ground. Tour captain Scotsman David Bedell-Sivright skippered the Test side for the only time during his two tours and was forced to rouse his team at half-time. The Lions responded with the Welsh leading the way. Wing Willie Llewellyn scored two tries while fly-half Percy Bush scored a try and dropped a goal. Number Eight Arthur 'Boxer' Harding kicked one conversion and New Zealand-born centre Arthur O'Brien, who also managed the tour, kicked another.

## WEDNESDAY 2nd JULY 1980

All-time Argentine great Hugo Porta faced the Lions as part of a SA Barbarians side at Kings Park, Durban. The presence of the fly-half could not prevent the Lions winning the match comfortably 25-14. Ireland fly-half Tony Ward scored 18 points with a try, two conversions and three penalties. The Lions scored two further tries through Scots Andy Irvine and Alan Tomes.

## SATURDAY 2nd JULY 2005

New Zealand fly-half Dan Carter racked up a record 33 points as the All Blacks cut loose in the second Test and wrapped up the series. The hosts were clearly fired up by the response of the Lions' management to the Brian O'Driscoll incident a week earlier; none more so than skipper Tana Umaga who scored the All Blacks' first try. That cancelled out an opening try from Gareth Thomas, who was captaining the Lions. The hosts then blew the Lions away with further tries from Richie McCaw, Sitiveni Sivivatu and two from Carter, who scored with nine of his ten attempts at goal.

## SATURDAY 3rd JULY 1993

For the first time since 1971 the Lions went into the final Test in New Zealand with the series still alive. High hopes engendered by the Lions' comprehensive victory the previous week were dashed as the All Blacks turned the tables brilliantly despite falling 10-0 behind early on to a Scott Gibbs try. Tries from skipper Sean Fitzpatrick, centre Frank Bunce and scrum-half Jon Preston allied with the boot of Grant Fox gave the hosts a 30-13 win.

## TUESDAY 4th JULY 1865

Alfred Shaw, co-manager of the 1888 tour, bowled out WG Grace in the Gentlemen v Players match at The Oval in London. It was the first time that Shaw had taken Grace's wicket in a match and he would take it on another 48 occasions, more times than any other bowler.

## SATURDAY 4th JULY 2009

The British & Irish Lions won their first Test match in eight years and eight attempts, restoring some pride with a 28-9 victory in the final rubber of the series against the Springboks. The score equalled the Lions' highest in South Africa and biggest winning margin versus the Springboks, which had been set in 1974. With the series over the Lions made eight changes while the hosts made 10. Two tries from Wales wing Shane Williams set the Lions on course for victory. Ugo Monye, playing on the other wing, scored another try while fly-half Stephen Jones kicked 13 points.

## SATURDAY 5th JULY 1980

The Lions kicked a record three dropped goals for a Tour match in South Africa as Western Province were thrashed at Newlands in Cape Town. Ireland fly-half Ollie Campbell kicked two of the dropped goals as part of his personal haul of 22 points in the match. Scotland full-back Andy Irvine kicked the other dropped goal and added a try as the Lions headed into the final week of the Tour and fourth Test with a confidence building 37-6 victory.

## SATURDAY 5th JULY 1997

The third and final Test at Ellis Park in Johannesburg proved a match too far for the Lions who went down 35-16 to a wounded Springbok side that was determined to avoid a Test whitewash on home soil. The Springboks scored four tries through Joost van der Westhuizen, Percy Montgomery, Andre Snyman and Pieter Roussow while the Lions could only muster a Matt Dawson effort in reply.

## WEDNESDAY 6th JULY 1904

England international Denys Dobson became the first man to be sent off while playing for the Lions. Referee Frank Moran dismissed Dobson for allegedly swearing at him after the award of a free kick to the opposition. In response, Lions captain David Bedell-Sivright led the entire team from the field. After 20 minutes of discussions the Lions resumed the match without Dobson. Although the Lions were now down to 13 men, Fred Jowett had already departed the field injured, they went on to beat Northern Districts 17-3.

## SATURDAY 6th JULY 2013

Warren Gatland's Lions team cut loose and clinched the Test series in style at ANZ Stadium in Sydney. The tourists capitalised on Will Genia's mistake at the kick off to score a try in the first minute through prop Alex Corbisiero. The front row then demolished the Wallaby scrum to set up a record 41-16 win over the Wallabies with Leigh Halfpenny kicking five penalties and three conversions. Jonathan Sexton, George North and Jamie Roberts all touched down in the second half as the Lions ran away with both match and the series.

## SATURDAY 7th JULY 2001

Two moments either side of half-time turned the second Test, and ultimately the series, in Australia's favour. The loss of flanker Richard Hill to Nathan Grey's cowardly elbow to the back of the head robbed the Lions of a key player and shortly after the restart Jonny Wilkinson's speculative pass was intercepted by Joe Roff who raced in for a score to revive the flagging Wallabies. The Lions had led 11-6 at half time with Neil Back having scored a try, however the score did not reflect their dominance. They were made to pay as Roff scored a second and Matt Burke touched down as part of his personal haul of 25 points in a 35-14 win that was the Lions' worst Test defeat in 28 years.

## SATURDAY 8th JULY 1989

Scrum-halves Rob Jones and Nick Farr-Jones lit the fuse for the "Battle of Ballymore" with a scrap in the first minute of the second Test. The Lions pack charged into the fray after Jones set the tone for a physical battle that saw the tourists dominate a ruffled Wallaby eight. Head Coach Ian McGeechan made five changes following the comprehensive defeat in the first Test. Amongst those coming in was Gloucester forward Mike Teague, who won the Player of the Series award despite missing the first rubber, and Rob Andrew who gave a commanding display from fly-half. Also selected was 23-year-old England centre Jeremy Guscott who scored the match winning try by re-gathering his own kick to touch down. The Lions had trailed until late on when a Gavin Hastings try put them into a lead that they extended to 19-12 to level the series in Brisbane.

## THURSDAY 9th JULY 1891

The Lions' first ever match on South African soil ended in a convincing 15-1 victory over a Cape Town XV at Newlands. The Lions scored four tries; two each for wings Randolph Aston and Paul Clauss, while fly-half William Wotherspoon kicked 11 points. Herbert Castens refereed the match while Hasie Versfeld had the honour of being the first South African to score a try against the Lions and his score was the only one the Lions were to concede on the tour.

## TUESDAY 9th JULY 1974

The 1974 Lions recorded another first as they took on the Leopards, a side made up of black players, in East London. The tourists ran out easy 56-10 winners with England wing Alan Morley scoring his one and only Lions try. The try was part of his world record haul of 479 first class tries. The Leopards also managed one try in reply, embarrassing the Springboks who had yet to pierce the Lions defence in the Test series.

## SATURDAY 9th JULY 1977

The Lions levelled the series at a match apiece after winning the second Test 13-9 at Lancaster Park in Christchurch. In a bad-tempered affair played on a heavy, muddy pitch the Lions had their forwards to thank for victory as the pack subdued the All Blacks eight. Welsh wing JJ Williams scored the only try of the match while captain Phil Bennett kicked three penalties. However, it was Welsh flanker Terry Cobner who led the forward effort after reminding the Lions in his pre-match speech match that: "You are not alone, because at three in the morning lights will be going on in the villages and towns of the valleys, and they will be listening on their radios and willing you on, and they will be with you every inch of the way. So remember when you are out there on that pitch, you are not alone."

## MONDAY 10th JULY 1916

A charging rhinoceros fatally gored 1904 tourist Denys Dobson in Africa. Dobson, who was a forward, played rugby for Oxford University, the Barbarians and England. He appeared 16 times, including all four Tests, on David Bedell-Sivright's Tour of Australia scoring two tries and having the misfortune to be the first Lion ever sent off. After his playing career was over he was posted as a Colonial Officer to Nyasaland.

## SATURDAY 10th JULY 1971

The All Blacks hit back to level the Test series with a 22-12 victory at Lancaster Park in Christchurch. New Zealand scored five tries, including a memorable 50-metre charge by flanker Ian Kirkpatrick, to end the Lions' 15-match unbeaten run.

ANDY IRVINE CLEARS, FLANKED BY TERRY COBNER (L) AND PHIL BENNETT (R)

## THURSDAY 10th JULY 2014

Scotland and Lions centre Scott Hastings joined the panel of BBC TV's *Question Time* as it debated Scottish independence in the run-up to the country's referendum. Also on the panel in Inverness, which contained no politicians, were singer and broadcaster Ricky Ross, journalist Joan Burnie and businessman Alan Savage. A BBC spokesman said: "The debate is not just between parties but has also involved every section of society in Scotland, and we hope we are reflecting that with tonight's panel."

## THURSDAY 11th JULY 1985

Jonathan Sexton was born in Dublin, Ireland. The fly-half was a key figure in Leinster's three Heineken Cup triumphs between 2009 and 2012. He was also a key figure in Ireland's 2014 Six Nations title-winning campaign a year after he had helped the Lions to a series victory in Australia. He played in all three Tests and his try in the final match opened the floodgates for a convincing Lions win.

## WEDNESDAY 12th JULY 1916

Johnnie Williams was killed in action during the taking of Mametz Wood at the Battle of the Somme aged 34. The wing was first capped by Wales in 1906 and scored 17 tries in 17 matches for his country, only finishing on the losing side twice. Williams was the Lions' top try scorer on the 1908 Tour of Australia and New Zealand with 12 scores in 19 appearances.

## SATURDAY 12th JULY 1980

Scottish full-back Andy Irvine's try in the final Test of the series took his Lions points tally to 274 in all matches, a record total for the team. Irvine toured three times playing in 42 matches and scoring 20 tries, 34 conversions, two dropped goals and 40 penalties for a record haul. The visitors won the fourth Test at Loftus Versfeld in Pretoria by 17-13 to salvage some pride and avoid becoming the first Lions side to suffer a Test whitewash in South Africa. Welsh prop Clive Williams and Irish flanker John O'Driscoll also touched down for the Lions with Irish fly-half Ollie Campbell kicking a conversion and a penalty.

## SATURDAY 13th JULY 1974

Willie John McBride's Lions became the first to win a series in South Africa since 1896 as they routed South Africa 26-9 in the third Test to take an unassailable 3-0 lead in the series. The second Battle of Boet Erasmus was won comprehensively by the Lions who forced the Springbok forwards to retreat from the fight. Welsh wing JJ Williams scored another two Test tries after Gordon Brown had barged over from a short lineout for the opener. Phil Bennett dropped two goals and Andy Irvine kicked another eight points, as the Lions became the first touring party to beat the Springboks on their home turf in the 20th century.

## THURSDAY 14th JULY 1932

Vivian Jenkins recorded his highest score for Glamorgan with 65 in a County Championship match against Surrey at The Oval in London. The Welsh full-back toured South Africa with the 1938 Lions. He kicked 50 points in 13 matches before his Tour was cut short by injury. In the first Test it was Jenkins who kicked nine of the Lions' 12 points, including landing a penalty from inside the tourists' own half.

## SATURDAY 14th JULY 2001

The 2001 series came down to one final lineout throw with less than two minutes on the clock. The Lions were thwarted when Justin Harrison stole the ball and deprived them the opportunity to score the converted try that would have snatched the final Test. The match at Stadium Australia was played in front of a crowd of 84,188, a record for a Lions Test, who witnessed the lead change hands several times. Jason Robinson and Jonny Wilkinson's scores cancelled out Daniel Herbert's two tries for the Wallabies. However, indiscipline cost the Lions with Matt Burke kicking five penalties to see Australia home 29-23.

## WEDNESDAY 15th JULY 1896

Cape Prime Minister Sir Gordon Sprigg entertained the Lions before their match with Western Province and although the team were under orders to restrict themselves to four tumblers of champagne there were suspicions that they over-indulged before being held 0-0.

## SATURDAY 15th JULY 1989

Australian wing David Campese's suicidal back pass gifted the Lions the only try of the third and final Test - and ultimately the series too. The Wallabies were leading 12-9 after an hour when Campese tried running the ball out from behind his own goal line. The maverick wing's attempted pass to Greg Martin was wayward allowing Ieuan Evans to pounce for the vital score. Two Gavin Hastings penalties extended the Lions lead and although Michael Lynagh reduced the deficit to 18-19 and the Wallabies fought until the end the Lions defence heroically held out. Finlay Calder's side became only the second Lions team to win a series after losing the first Test.

## SATURDAY 16th JULY 1983

All Black wing Stu Wilson ran in a hat-trick of tries as New Zealand put the Lions to the sword in the fourth Test at Eden Park in Auckland. The 38-6 scoreline is the worst defeat suffered by the Lions in any match and completed a 4-0 series win for the hosts. Having already clinched the series the All Blacks unleashed their attacking instincts in the Tour finale. A rampant New Zealand pack dominated the match and there were further tries for Andy Haden, Jock Hobbs and Allan Hewson – who also kicked 14 points. Ollie Campbell and Gwyn Evans kicked a penalty each for the sorry Lions who ended a poor Tour on disastrous note.

## SATURDAY 17th JULY 1971

Welsh wing Gerald Davies scored four tries as the Lions demolished Hawkes Bay 25-6 at McLean Park in Napier. It was another match marred by violence on the Tour with the hosts unable to match the visitors at rugby so resorting to foul play instead. England hooker John Pullin was one victim as he was badly hurt by a punch. Welsh fly-half Barry John made his disapproval known and taunted the opposition by sitting on the ball, passing it behind his back or pretending to offer it to the Hawkes Bay pack only to kick it to touch before they could take it. The dirty tactics of the home team failed to disrupt the Lions who once again ran out convincing winners.

## SATURDAY 18th JULY 1959

The prodigious boot of New Zealand full-back Don Clarke handed the Lions a bitter defeat and prompted a debate about the value of penalty goals and tries that would eventually lead to the value of a try being increased to four points. The Lions had outscored the All Blacks four tries to nil but lost the first Test 18-17 with Clarke kicking all the home side's points. Two tries from centre Malcolm Price and one apiece for wings Tony O'Reilly and Peter Jackson looked to have won the match for the Lions as they took a 17-9 lead. However, Clarke finished with six penalties - five from long distances - and his mighty kicking snatched the Test.

## MONDAY 19th JULY 1943

Irish flanker Robert Alexander was killed in action while serving near Catania in Sicily with the Royal Inniskilling Fusiliers. Five years earlier Alexander had toured South Africa with Sam Walker's Lions team. He played in 14 matches including all three Tests and scored six tries. Alexander, who was 32 years old at the time of his death, was a double international who had represented Ireland at both rugby union and cricket.

## MONDAY 20th JULY 1891

The performance of the Griqualand West team that restricted the British & Irish Lions to a 3-0 victory was rewarded with the first ever Currie Cup. The trophy had been donated by shipping magnate Donald Currie who instructed the Lions to award the cup to whichever team gave them the best match. A Bill MacLagan try and Arthur Rotherham penalty gave the Lions victory but the hosts' performance earned them the cup, which is now the trophy for South Africa's premier domestic competition.

## WEDNESDAY 20th JULY 1977

The Lions beat the Junior All Blacks 19-9 in atrocious conditions at Athletic Park in Wellington. The enduring image of the match was England prop Fran Cotton caked in mud at a lineout. The 'Mudman' image has since become one of the most iconic images of rugby union. Cotton was on the second of his three Lions tours during which he won seven Test caps.

## SATURDAY 21st JULY 1888

The Shaw and Shrewsbury tourists beat Ballarat 5-4 in a Victorian Rules match at the Saxon Paddock Reserve. The victory avenged a 4-1 defeat to the same team the previous day. In all the original Lions team played 19 matches of Victorian Rules football winning six, drawing one and losing 12.

## TUESDAY 21st JULY 1908

A strong Lions side containing seven Test players beat a local Maori side 24-3 in an unofficial 'picnic' match in Rotorua just five days before the final international with the All Blacks. Although the match was won handsomely with two tries for full-back John Dykes and one apiece for Herbert Laxon, James 'Tuan' Jones, Rowland Griffiths and Pat McEvedy it was less than ideal preparation for the final Test.

## SATURDAY 21st JULY 1962

The local referee, who said he was unsighted, condemned the Lions to a narrow loss in the second Test against South Africa, when he controversially ruled out Keith Rowlands' last-minute try. Springbok fly-half Keith Oxlee kicked the only points for the game to give his side a 3-0 win.

## SATURDAY 22nd JULY 1899

A virtuoso performance from Welsh threequarter Gwyn Nicholls helped the Lions level the series with a comprehensive 11-0 win in Brisbane. Matthew Mullineux was missing from the Lions side due to injury so England forward Frank Stout led the tourists into the second Test. The absence of the captain made no difference to the Lions as Nicholls created tries for Charlie Adamson and Alan Ayre-Smith before adding the third himself.

## SATURDAY 23rd JULY 1904

Wales fly-half Percy Bush set the individual points record for a Lion in a Test match with 11 as the Lions cut loose in the second half of the second Test against Australia. The Wallabies had led 3-0 at half time through a Bluey Burdon try. However, the tourists dominated after the break with Bush, Willie Llewellyn and Arthur O'Brien scoring tries while the fly-half added two dropped goals for a 17-3 win.

## SATURDAY 23rd JULY 1938

Wing Elvet Jones scored a hat-trick of tries as the Lions beat Rhodesia 45-11 at the Hartsfield Ground in Bulawayo. It was Jones' second hat-trick of the tour, the first came in the 19-10 victory over South-Western Districts, and he scored 10 tries in all on the trip.

## THURSDAY 24th JULY 1924

Scotland wing Ian Smith scored a brace of tries as the Lions outclassed Rhodesia by 16-3 at the Salisbury Sports Ground.

## SATURDAY 25th JULY 1908

The Lions paid the price for a week of merrymaking in Rotorua as they were thrashed 29-0 in the final Test of the series. The score remained the Lions' worst defeat until 1983 and the nine tries conceded remains a record. All Black centre Frank Mitchinson was their main tormentor with a hat-trick while Jimmy Hunter, Bob Deans, Frank Glasgow, Harold Hayward, Bolla Francis and George Gillett all touched down. The defeat would have been much heavier still if the home team had managed to convert more than one of its tries.

## FRIDAY 26th JULY 1918

The award of a bar to the Military Cross of Lions centre James 'Tuan' Jones, won while serving in France as a Captain in the Royal Army Medical Corps, was announced in *The London Gazette*. The citation reads: "He was in charge of an advanced dressing-station, and when the village had been temporarily evacuated he was entirely responsible for the getting away safely of many of the wounded. Throughout the ten days of the battle he displayed the most conspicuous ability, cool courage and devotion to duty."

## SATURDAY 26th JULY 1930

New Zealand took a grip on the 1930 series with a 15-10 victory over the Lions at Eden Park in Auckland. The scores were level at half-time after Lions centre Harry Bowcott's brilliant solo try had been cancelled out by Fred Lucas. All Black flanker Hugh McLean scored two tries on his debut while Mark Nicholls added a dropped goal but the Lions hit back with Carl Aarvold scoring under the posts and Brian Black converting.

## MONDAY 27th JULY 1908

Bristol forward Percy Down fell into Auckland Harbour and had to be rescued by All Blacks George Gillett and Bolla Francis. The Lions were sent off by hundreds of well-wishers as they boarded the steamer *Victoria* bound for Sydney. Down was "bending to shake hands with a lady acquaintance" when he fell over the rail. His rescue caused a delay after which their ship departed although it was still minus one squad member. England and Oxford University centre Henry 'Jumbo' Vassall failed to arrive in time for departure as he was "visiting lady friends". He made his own way to Sydney where he was reunited with the rest of the squad.

## SATURDAY 27th JULY 1968

South Africa eased to a 19-6 win at Ellis Park to complete a 3-0 series victory with one match drawn. The Lions points came from two Tom Kiernan penalties. The kicks meant that the Lions captain and full-back had scored 35 of his side's 38 points during the series. Kiernan kicked 11 penalties in the four Tests and also converted Willie John McBride's try in the opener.

## SATURDAY 27th JULY 1974

Captain Willie John McBride was denied victory in his 17th and final Lions Test and his team were prevented from leaving South Africa with a 100% record when Fergus Slattery's last-minute try was disallowed. South African referee Max Baise blew up early denying Slattery the score and the Lions a final victory, later telling hooker Bobby Windsor: "Look boys, I have to live here." The final Test finished in a 13-13 draw to leave the 1974 Lions undefeated as their skipper bowed out with a record number of Test appearances for the side as well as setting the record for the Lions in all Tour matches with 70.

## TUESDAY 28th JULY 1891

The Lions completed their preparations for their first ever Test match with a 21-0 victory over Eastern Province at the Crusaders Ground in Port Elizabeth. The win ensured that the tourists remained unbeaten when they met the Springboks for the first time two days later.

## WEDNESDAY 29th JULY 1936

Rosslyn Park wing Jim Unwin scored five of the team's 15 tries as the Lions' point scoring record was improved with a 62-0 win over Pacific Railways at the Estadio GEBA in Buenos Aires.

## TUESDAY 29th JULY 1941

1903 Lion and royal confidant Louis Greig accompanied Prince George on a top-secret wartime journey to the USA. The pair flew across the Atlantic Ocean, the first time a member of the Royal Family had ever made the trip by air, to visit RAF training schools.

## THURSDAY 30th JULY 1891

The British & Irish Lions met South Africa in the first ever Test match played by either side. Scot Bill MacLagan led the Lions to a 4-0 victory over the Springboks, who were captained by the ubiquitous Herbert Castens, who was a regular presence as opponent, coach and referee during the tour. Wing Randolph Aston and forward Thomas Whitaker scored the Lions tries while scrum-half Arthur Rotherham added a conversion.

## FRIDAY 30th JULY 1954

The opening ceremony of the British Empire and Commonwealth Games took place at the Empire Stadium in Vancouver, Canada. Wales and Lions wing Ken Jones was amongst the medal winners in the athletics as he won bronze in the 220-yard race.

## SATURDAY 31st JULY 1971

The Lions took a 2-1 lead in the Test series after beating New Zealand 13-3 in the third Test at Athletic Park in Wellington. The Lions gave debuts to forwards Gordon Brown and Derek Quinnell, the latter was still uncapped for Wales, and took advantage of a strong wind to rack up a 13-0 advantage. Fly-half Barry John dropped a goal before Gareth Edwards put Gerald Davies away for a try down the blind side. John converted that try as well as one of his own after he linked up with Edwards. All Black full-back Laurie Mains scored a try after the break but the Lions defence held firm to secure a vital victory.

# THE BRITISH & IRISH LIONS
## *On This Day*

SINCE 1888

# AUGUST

## WEDNESDAY 1st AUGUST 2001

The South African Post Office issued a stamp featuring Captain Thomas Crean VC as part of its commemorations for the Second Boer War. Crean toured South Africa with Jonny Hammond's team in 1896 and stayed on in Johannesburg to work as a doctor. After the Second Boer War broke out he enlisted in the Imperial Light Horse and was involved in the Relief of Mafeking and the Relief of Ladysmith before being wounded at the Battle of Elandslaagte. After he recovered he won a Victoria Cross for his actions at the Battle of Tygerkloof in 1901, the following year he was wounded again and invalided back to England.

## SATURDAY 2nd AUGUST 1924

A 12-12 draw with Transvaal at the Wanderers in Johannesburg heralded the longest winless run in Lions matches. It would be eight games and a full calendar month before the Lions registered another victory as Ronald Cove-Smith's side struggled with an injury crisis. A 3-3 draw with Natal was the best result in a sequence that saw the Lions lose the opening two Tests of the series as well as matches against Orange Free State, Witwatersrand and Pretoria. The team finally broke the run with a victory over Cape Colony.

## FRIDAY 2nd AUGUST 1985

Stephen Ferris was born in Portadown, Northern Ireland. The flanker won 35 Ireland caps and was part of Declan Kidney's Grand Slam team in 2009. Later that year he was selected to join the Lions in South Africa. Ferris scored a try against the Golden Lions before a knee injury cut his Tour short.

## FRIDAY 3rd AUGUST 1973

Jules Malfroy died in Great Shelford, Cambridgeshire aged 71. The diminutive Malfroy was born in New Zealand but won a scholarship to study law at Cambridge University in 1925. The scrum-half won a rugby Blue in 1926 and was one of six Cambridge University players to join the Lions on the Tour of Argentina in 1927 but was not selected for any of the international fixtures. During World War Two he attained the rank of Wing Commander in the RAF.

## WEDNESDAY 3rd AUGUST 1977

The famous Pontypool front row of Graham Price, Bobby Windsor and Charlie Faulkner packed down together as Lions for the first time as Counties/Thames Valley were beaten 35-10 in Pukekohe. The trio, who were known collectively as the Viet Gwent, would play together twice more on the Tour in the matches against Bay of Plenty and Fiji.

## SATURDAY 4th AUGUST 1962

A moment of madness from England fly-half Richard Sharp allowed the Springboks to snatch victory in the third Test at Newlands in Cape Town. The sides were locked together at 3-3 in the closing stages of the match when Welsh hooker Bryn Meredith took a scrum against the head near the Lions line. Sharp ran instead of kicking clear and his hospital pass to Ken Jones gave the wing no chance of holding on to the ball. South Africa fly-half Keith Oxlee pounced on the loose ball and ran in the try, which he converted to make the final score 8-3 to the hosts. Earlier in the match Sharp had opened the scoring with a dropped goal that was cancelled out by Oxlee's penalty.

## SATURDAY 5th AUGUST 1899

Scottish wing Alf Bucher became the first Lion to score two tries in a Test match as the tourists took a 2-1 lead in the series with a narrow 11-10 win at the Sydney Cricket Ground. Bucher's scores along with a try for Alec Timms and two Charlie Adamson conversions looked to have put the visitors in command. However, Australian centre Lonnie Spragg's personal haul of 10 points reduced the deficit and scrum-half Igantius O'Donnell almost won it for the Wallabies with a last-minute attempt at a dropped goal that drifted wide.

## SATURDAY 6th AUGUST 1910

The Lions went down 14-10 in the opening rubber of the Test series at the Wanderers in Johannesburg. The tourists had rallied from 11-3 down to come within a point thanks to a Jack Jones dropped goal and a Jack Spoors try. The Springboks made the game safe when 'Cocky' Hahn gathered Dougie Morkel's kick to cross for a try.

## SATURDAY 6th AUGUST 1938

South Africa won the opening Test of the series 26-12 at Ellis Park in Johannesburg despite the efforts of Vivian Jenkins. The Welsh full-back kicked three penalties, including a monster from eight yards inside the Lions' own half. Flanker Russell Taylor had opened the scoring for the Lions but the Springboks scored four tries to run out convincing winners. Wing Dai Williams scored two while Tony Harris and Fanie Louw got one apiece and Gerrie Brand kicked 14 points.

## SATURDAY 6th AUGUST 1955

A huge crowd at Ellis Park was treated to a classic in the first Test of the 1955 series with the visitors triumphing 23-22. The official attendance for the match was 95,000, but some estimates put the true figure at closer to 110,000 due to the thriving black market in forged tickets. The Lions scored a record five tries in a Test, which has since been equalled but not bettered, while South Africa touched down four times. English centre Jeff Butterfield created a classic try for Irish wing Cecil Pedlow before scoring one himself. Nevertheless the Lions trailed 11-8 at half-time and things looked bleak when they lost flanker Reg Higgins to injury shortly after the restart. The 14 remaining Lions scored further tries through Cliff Morgan, Tony O'Reilly and Jim Greenwood. South Africa still had a chance to snatch victory with the final kick of the match but Jack van der Schyff failed with a conversion attempt. Many Lions fans and players could not bear to watch the kick with O'Reilly later saying his eyes were closed because, "I was merely in direct communication with the Vatican".

## SUNDAY 7th AUGUST 1927

The Lions racked up their biggest ever Test win with a 46-0 over Argentina at the Estadio GEBA in Buenos Aires. English wing Carl Aarvold scored four tries while Scottish inside centre Robert Kelly touched down twice. Lions captain and Number Eight David MacMyn, flanker George McIlwanie, prop Charles Payne and fly-half Roger Spong also scored tries while outside centre Ernest Hammett kicked 16 points. The victory put the Lions 2-0 up in the four-match series.

## SATURDAY 7th AUGUST 1948

Welsh wing Ken Jones won an Olympic silver medal as part of the Great Britain quartet that finished behind the USA in the 4x100 metres relay at the London Games. Blaenavon-born Jones had made his Wales debut a year earlier and would tour Australasia with the Lions in 1950. He scored 17 tries in 44 appearances for Wales and another two in his three Lions Tests. His speed as a sprinter was in evidence as he combined with Lewis Jones to score with one of the all-time great tries in the third Test against New Zealand.

## SATURDAY 7th AUGUST 1971

Welsh wing John Bevan equalled Tony O'Reilly's record of 17 tries during the New Zealand leg of a Tour when he touched down in the 11-5 victory over North Auckland. Bevan, who was nicknamed 'The Ox', also scored a try against New South Wales to take his total to 18 for the tour.

## TUESDAY 8th AUGUST 1882

Arthur Shrewsbury scored 207 for Nottinghamshire in a County match against Surrey at Kennington Oval in London. It was the first double century ever scored for Notts and the second-wicket stand of 289 he shared with Billy Barnes was a first class record at the time. Shrewsbury's score helped Notts to victory by an innings and 189 runs over their hosts. Shrewsbury was one of the greatest English batsmen of his generation. He toured Australia four times as a cricketer before organising the first British rugby Tour to Australia and New Zealand in 1888 along with Notts and England bowler Alfred Shaw.

## SATURDAY 9th AUGUST 1930

The All Blacks clinched the Test series with a convincing win in the final rubber at Athletic Park, Wellington. The match was one too far for the Lions and having won the first Test and run New Zealand close in the next two they were swept aside 22-8 by the hosts' forward power. The All Blacks ran in four tries and in reply the Lions could only muster a solitary effort from wing Tony Novis.

## TUESDAY 10th AUGUST 1875

Hugh Gray was born in North Berwick, Scotland. The forward played for Cambridge University and Coventry and was invited to attend Scotland trials although he was never capped for his country. Nevertheless he was invited to tour Australia in 1899 winning two Test caps. In all he played 16 times for the Lions and scored two tries.

## TUESDAY 10th AUGUST 1971

A 20-14 victory over Bay of Plenty for the midweek side ensured that the Lions completed their non-international matches unbeaten in New Zealand. Irish centre Mike Gibson, who captained the side at the Domain, and Scottish wing Alistair Biggar scored a try each. Full-back Bob Hiller kicked a conversion and three penalties while fly-half Barry John dropped a goal to maintain his record of scoring on every one of his Tour appearances.

## TUESDAY 11th AUGUST 1891

The Lions registered the biggest win of the 1891 Tour with a 25-0 victory over Pietermaritzburg.

## SATURDAY 12th AUGUST 1899

Lions captain Matthew Mullineux upset his hosts with his remarks at the post-match banquet after his side had completed a 3-1 win in the Test series against Australia. Mullineux bemoaned some of the dark arts prevalent in Australian rugby at the time including pushing in the lineout and elbowing in the scrums. Mullineux said: "Please blot these things from your football for instead of developing all that is manly they bring forth all that is unmanly." Earlier the Lions had triumphed 13-0 victory at the Sydney Cricket Ground with Durham scrum-half Charlie Adamson scoring 10 points with a try, two conversions and a penalty.

## WEDNESDAY 12th AUGUST 1908

James Baxter won a silver medal for sailing at the London Olympics. Baxter was part of the crew of the yacht Mouchette that won the silver for Great Britain. Baxter also represented England at rugby union, winning three caps in 1900, and was manager of the Lions tours of Argentina in 1927 and New Zealand three years later.

## SATURDAY 13th AUGUST 1904

The first ever Test match between the British & Irish Lions and New Zealand took place at Athletic Park, Wellington. The match attracted a crowd of 20,000, which included the Governor of New Zealand, the country's prime minister and most of his government. The hosts won the match 9-3 thanks to two second-half tries from wing Duncan McGregor. The first half had finished level after Billy Wallace's penalty for the All Blacks was cancelled out by one from Lions captain Arthur 'Boxer' Harding.

## SATURDAY 13th AUGUST 1910

English wing Maurice Neale scored a hat-trick of tries as the Lions beat Border 30-10 in East London. Neale would finish the 1910 Tour as leading try scorer with nine, including the winning score in the second Test against the Springboks.

## SATURDAY 13th AUGUST 1938

Everard Jackson made his 11th and final appearance for New Zealand as the All Blacks beat Australia 14-6 in Sydney. The prop was the son of 1908 Lion Fred Jackson who stayed on in New Zealand at the end of his tour. The elder Jackson played four matches on Tour scoring one try and kicking a further 12 points. After settling in New Zealand Jackson switched codes and won a rugby league cap for his adopted country in a 52-20 defeat to Great Britain in Auckland.

## SATURDAY 13th AUGUST 1977

All Black Number Eight Lawrie Knight's late try broke Lions' hearts and clinched the Test series for New Zealand with a 10-9 win at Eden Park. In a match they needed to win to level the series the tourists had led 9-3 at the break. Scotland scrum-half Dougie Morgan scored all the Lions points adding a penalty and a conversion to a well-worked try that had involved Fran Cotton, Bill Beaumont, Graham Price and Steve Fenwick in the build-up. The Lions forwards dominated the match but New Zealand full-back Bevan Wilson kicked a penalty in each half to keep them in touch before Knight provided the killer blow.

## SUNDAY 14th AUGUST 1927

Scottish wing Edward Taylor bagged a hat-trick as the Lions beat Argentina 34-3 to take a 3-0 lead in the international series. The tourists scored seven tries in all with inside centre Arthur Hamilton-Smythe crossing twice while flanker George McIlwanie and scrum-half Peter Douty got one apiece. Outside centre Ernest Hammett kicked 13 points.

## SATURDAY 14th AUGUST 1971

The Lions sealed a series win in New Zealand for the only time in their history with a 14-14 draw in the fourth Test at Eden Park in Auckland. The match was a tight, tense affair and the Lions fell behind 8-0 early on. Fly-half Barry John got them on the scoreboard with a penalty before English flanker Peter Dixon crashed over for a try from a lineout. John converted the try to level the scores at the break. In the second half the Lions edged ahead through another John penalty and again through JPR Williams' dropped goal only to be pegged back by the All Blacks both times. However, a draw was enough for the Lions who clinched a historic 2-1 series win.

## WEDNESDAY 15th AUGUST 1888

Robert Seddon, the first ever captain of the Lions, was tragically drowned in a boating accident near Maitland, New South Wales. The 28-year-old had stayed on in the town, along with Andrew Stoddart and Jack Anderton, following a Victorian Rules match the previous day while the rest of the tourists took the train to Newcastle. Hundreds attended his funeral, which took place the following day in Maitland. One newspaper report said: "He had made himself exceedingly popular during the time he had been in the colonies, and his death has caused a painful sensation in athletic circles in Sydney."

## MONDAY 15th AUGUST 1927

Despite having played an international match the previous day the Lions returned to the Gimnasia y Esgrima in Buenos Aries and beat Combinado Clubes 29-3 for a second victory in less than 48 hours. The match was refereed by 1904 Lion Tommy Vile who travelled with the team and took charge of all their fixtures.

## SATURDAY 16th AUGUST 1924

The Lions lost the first Test 3-7 to South Africa in Durban. The Springboks took advantage of having the wind and sun at their backs to take a 7-0 lead in the fist half though a Hans Aucamp and Bennie Osler dropped goal. Despite losing centre Reg Maxwell with a dislocated shoulder the Lions improved in the second half but could only manage a solitary try through scrum-half Herbert Whitley.

## TUESDAY 16th AUGUST 1977

The 'Bad News Tour' of 1977 finished on a flat note with defeat to Fiji on the way home from New Zealand. Fiji won their first, and to date only, match against the Lions 25-21 in front of 20,000 at Buckhurst Park in Suva. The home side scored five tries with flanker Vuata Narisia touching down twice while prop Josefa Rauto, wing Joape Kuinikoro and hooker Atonio Racika also crossed for scores. The Lions hit back with tries for captain Phil Bennett, who was playing on the wing, Bill Beaumont and David Burcher but came up short.

## TUESDAY 17th AUGUST 1858

Tom Banks was born in Salford, Lancashire. Banks was a versatile player who began his rugby career as half back while studying medicine at Edinburgh University. While at Edinburgh he won the university's Long-Distance Swimming Championships. Banks returned to England and joined Swinton rugby club where he featured in both the backs and forwards. He joined the Shaw and Shrewsbury Tour of 1888 playing in seven matches and scoring a try against Otago in the second ever fixture played by the Lions.

## THURSDAY 18th AUGUST 1983

Granville Coghlan died aged 76. The giant English lock toured Argentina with David MacMyn's 'Lost Lions' of 1927. The Lions made a clean sweep of the four internationals with Coghlan featuring in the second and final Tests of the series, which were won by a combined score of 89-0, and scored a try in the last match. Despite his experience with the Lions and winning a rugby Blue at Cambridge University he was never capped by England.

## SATURDAY 19th AUGUST 1876

Alan Ayre-Smith was born in Richmond, England. The forward played rugby for Guy's Hospital in London and was selected to tour Australia in 1899. He played in 17 of the 20 matches on the Tour scoring tries against Rockhampton and in the second Test against the Wallabies. He played in all four Tests against Australia but was never capped for England.

## SATURDAY 19th AUGUST 1899

English forward Alan Ayre-Smith celebrated his 23rd birthday by helping beat Victoria 30-0 in Melbourne in the final match of the 1899 tour. It was the Lions' 17th victory in 20 matches on the trip.

## SATURDAY 19th AUGUST 1950

Welsh full-back Lewis Jones stole the show as the Lions outclassed Australia 19-6 at The Gabba in Brisbane. Jones was one of a record 10 Welshman in the Lions side for the first Test. He scored 16 of the Lions' 19 points, including a full house of all methods of scoring, the only Lion to ever achieve this in a Test match. Jones scored a try, two penalties, two conversions and a monster 50-yard dropped goal. His total of 16 points was also a record for one player in an international at the time.

## SATURDAY 20th AUGUST 1955

Springbok wing Tom Van Vollenhoven scored a brilliant hat-trick as South Africa thrashed the Lions 25-9 at Newlands in Cape Town. The rampant Springboks scored seven tries in all, six coming in the second half, with Van Vollenhoven who had been moved from centre to the wing, scoring the first three. Of the best Lions fly-half Cliff Morgan said: "He received a pass on the blind side of a scrum from Tommy Gentles with almost no room to move. His only option was to swerve infield, which he did marvellously. He then shaped to go outside Angus Cameron, who he beat completely as he moved to go inside. Finally, with another swerve, he was in under the posts. Clinical and brilliant." South Africa's other tries came from Theuns Briers, Roy Dryburgh, Wilf Rosenberg and Dawie Ackermann. Bryn Meredith and Jeff Butterfield touched down for the Lions.

## TUESDAY 20th AUGUST 1957

Twins Jim and Finlay Calder were born in Haddington, Scotland. The brothers both played at flanker and went on to win caps for both Scotland and the British & Irish Lions. Although the same age the twins' international careers did not overlap and they did not feature in the same Scotland or Lions teams. Jim won 27 caps for Scotland, scoring the vital try as they clinched the 1984 Grand Slam against France at Murrayfield. In 1983 he toured New Zealand with the Lions playing in seven matches and winning one Test cap. Finlay captained both his country and the Lions. Under his leadership the tourists won the 1989 series 2-1 becoming only the second Lions side to triumph after losing the first Test.

## SUNDAY 21st AUGUST 1927

Wing Carl Aarvold starred with a hat-trick of tries as the Lions completed their unbeaten Tour of Argentina in style. The tourists won the fourth and final Test 43-0 in Buenos Aires. The Lions scored 11 tries in all with Robert Kelly grabbing two while Granville Coghlan, George McIlwanie, David MacMyn, Roger Spong, Wilf Sobey and Guy Wilson all touched down. Aarvold finished with eight tries from four international matches on the tour.

## TUESDAY 21st AUGUST 1945

Acting Squadron Leader Charles Vesey Boyle was awarded the Distinguished Flying Cross just days after completing his 101st operational flight while serving with the Royal Air Force during World War Two. The Ireland wing travelled to Argentina with the Lions in 1936 on one of the 'Forgotten Tours' and two years later went to South Africa winning two Test caps on an official tour.

## SATURDAY 22nd AUGUST 1896

The Lions forwards dominated the second Test scoring three tries as a 17-8 victory at the Wanderers in Johannesburg put them 2-0 up in the series. Tries from Alexander Todd, Tom Crean and Froude Hancock helped the tourists to a 13-0 lead. However, Theo Samuels had the honour of scoring the Springboks' first ever Test try and the wing added the second soon afterwards. Lions centre Osbert Mackie made the game safe with a late dropped goal.

## SATURDAY 23rd AUGUST 1924

The Lions fell to a record 17-0 defeat in the second Test against South Africa. The Springboks scored four tries without reply through Kenny Starke, Phil Mostert, Jack van Druten and captain Pierre Albertyn. Fly-half Benny Osler added two conversions.

## MONDAY 24th AUGUST 1931

As the British economy struggled against the backdrop of the Great Depression Labour Prime Minister Ramsay MacDonald agreed to form a national government composed of "men from all parties" with the specific aim of balancing the budget and restoring confidence. Amongst the key figures behind the scenes that had helped make the national government possible were journalist Howell Arthur Gwynne, who had the ear of Conservative leader Stanley Baldwin, and 1903 Lion Louis Grieg, who counselled MacDonald.

## SATURDAY 25th AUGUST 1962

England's Dickie Jeeps was made captain in honour of his final Lions Test. It was Jeeps' 13th Test appearance for the tourists setting a record that has only been surpassed by Willie John McBride and is unlikely to be equalled again in the modern era. An unsentimental South African side marked the occasion with a 34-14 rout that completed a 3-0 series win, with one match drawn. It was a record score for the Springboks in South Africa as was fly-half Keith Oxlee's contribution of 16 points.

## WEDNESDAY 26th AUGUST 1903

The first Test of the 1903 series in South Africa saw Scotsmen captaining both sides as well as refereeing the match. David Bedell-Sivright led the Lions at the Wanderers in Johannesburg while his former Scotland teammate Alex Frew had taken over as Springbok skipper. Bill Donaldson, another former Scotland international, officiated a match that ended in a 10-10 stalemate.

## SATURDAY 26th AUGUST 1950

The Lions swept Australia aside 24-3 in the second Test in Sydney. Ireland second row Jimmy Nelson ran in two of the team's five tries with Jackie Kyle, Roy John and Ranald MacDonald scoring the others. Lewis Jones kicked a penalty and a conversion with John Robins adding another two conversions.

## SATURDAY 27th AUGUST 1910

The Lions moved flanker Charles 'Cherry' Pillman to fly-half for the second Test and were rewarded as he led them to an 8-3 victory in Port Elizabeth. Springbok captain Billy Millar said: "I confidently assert that if ever a man can have been said to have won an international match through his unorthodox and lonehanded efforts, it can be said of the inspired, black-haired Pillman I played against on the Crusader ground."

## SATURDAY 27th AUGUST 1966

Tries from Ireland Number Eight Ronnie Lamont and Wales fly-half David Watkins gave the Lions parity at half-time in the third Test in Christchurch. However, an error strewn second half allowed New Zealand to run out convincing 19-6 winners and take a 3-0 stranglehold on the series. All Blacks flanker Waka Nathan scored two tries with wing Tony Steel adding another.

## SATURDAY 28th AUGUST 1886

Nottinghamshire clinched their fourth County Championship in a row under the captaincy of Alfred Shaw, co-manager of the 1888 tour. The county's final match of the season ended in a draw with Kent at Trent Bridge but earlier results had been enough to claim the title once again.

## SATURDAY 29th AUGUST 1891

William and Edward Bromet became the first brothers to play for the Lions in a Test match when they lined up for the second Test at the Eclectic Cricket Ground in Kimberley. English full-back William Mitchell scored the only points of the match as the Lions won 3-0. Mitchell kicked a goal from mark in front of 3,000 spectators to put the tourists two up in the three match series.

## SATURDAY 29th AUGUST 1896

The Lions dominated the second-half of the third Test at Athletic Ground in Kimberley winning 9-3 to take an unassailable 3-0 lead in the Test series. The Springboks led at the break through a Percy Jones try. Fred Byrne kicked a four-point dropped goal, to put the tourists into the lead, and then converted Osbert Mackie's try to complete the victory.

## SATURDAY 29th AUGUST 1959

New Zealand took an invulnerable 3-0 lead in the Test series with a convincing 22-8 win over the British & Irish Lions at Lancaster Park in Christchurch. After two narrow wins the All Blacks showed their class to seal the series. New Zealand wing Ralph Caulton scored two tries with Colin Meads and Spider Urbahn adding one apiece. Full-back Don Clarke continued his astonishing form against the Lions with 10 points including a dropped goal with his weaker foot. Centre Dave Hewitt scored a try for the Lions with Number Eight John Faull kicking five points.

## SATURDAY 30th AUGUST 1924

The Lions ended the worst winless streak in their history with a 13-3 victory over Cape Province in Kimberley. It had been eight matches and a calendar month since the tourists had last recorded a win. Injuries had been a major cause of this dismal run and the situation prompted the call up of Ireland fly-half Bill Cunningham for the Cape Province match. Cunningham had won eight Ireland caps between 1920 and 1923 before emigrating to South Africa and was working as a dentist in Johannesburg when the Lions sent for him.

## SATURDAY 30th AUGUST 1930

The Lions lost to the Wallabies for only the second time as the hosts squeezed home by a point in Sydney in a one-off Test match. Australia scored tries through wing Gordon McGhie and scrum-half Sid Malcolm while the visitors replied through a Tony Novis score that captain Doug Prentice converted.

## WEDNESDAY 31st AUGUST 1881

Frank Hulme was born in Oxton, England. The scrum-half was capped four times for England between 1903 and 1905 and was selected to join David Bedell-Sivright's side in Australia and New Zealand in 1904. His six appearances all came on the Australian leg of the Tour and all ended in victories. Hulme scored his one Lions try against Metropolitan and won a cap in the 17-0 first Test win against the Wallabies.

# THE BRITISH & IRISH LIONS
## *On This Day*

SINCE 1888

# SEPTEMBER

## SATURDAY 1st SEPTEMBER 1973

Simon Shaw was born in Nairobi, Kenya. The England lock was 35 years old when he was selected for the 2009 Tour to South Africa. It was his third Lions Tour and he finally won a Test cap 12 years after first visiting South Africa on Tour with the Lions. Shaw was also called up as injury cover on the 2005 Tour after Irish lock Malcolm O'Kelly withdrew due to a groin injury. In total Shaw featured in 19 Lions matches and scored two tries, both against Northern Free State in 1997. He played in the final two Tests of the 2009 series and was awarded man of the match in the first.

## FRIDAY 2nd SEPTEMBER 1904

Two days after a 5-0 victory over New South Wales had completed the Australian leg of the Tour with a 100% record, the Sydney Morning Herald gave the Lions a glowing review: "It is not too much to say that the visiting team has done a great deal to place football as it is known here in the category of scientific games... Our British visitors have shown us that skill and success are far from being necessarily related to violence. They have shown the rugby game in its perfection, shown it as calling forth the highest power of the athlete in the avoidance of danger as well as in the overcoming of obstacles."

## SATURDAY 2nd SEPTEMBER 1905

Blair Swannell won his one and only Australian cap as the Wallabies went down 14-3 to New Zealand at Tahuna Park in Dunedin. Swannell had previously won six caps against the Wallabies over the course of the 1899 and 1904 Lions tours, he also played one Lions Test versus New Zealand. In all Swannell played 17 times for the Lions scoring one try, against Australia in Sydney in 1904. Swannell, along with David Bedell-Sivright and Dr Sidney Crowther, stayed on in Australia at the end of the 1904 tour. He settled in Sydney and joined the Northern Suburbs club. However, Australian captain Herbert Moran said: "Swannell was a bad influence in Sydney football... his conception of rugby was one of trained violence."

## SATURDAY 3rd SEPTEMBER 1910

The Lions played most of the final Test against the Springboks with only 14 men after the early loss of English full-back Stanley Williams. The tourists could not overcome the handicap and were well beaten with South Africa winning 21-5 to take the series 2-1. Outside half Jack Spoors scored the Lions try, which was converted by Charles Pillman. Spoors scored a try in all three of the Test matches and his record of scoring in his first three Lions internationals has only been equalled by Jeff Butterfield.

## SATURDAY 3rd SEPTEMBER 1955

Welsh fly-half Cliff Morgan was dubbed "Morgan the Magnificent" by the local press after his tactical kicking masterclass guided the Lions to a 9-6 victory in the third Test against South Africa. In the first Test to be staged at Pretoria's Loftus Versfeld Stadium Morgan's boot ensured the Lions won the territorial battle while the forwards took on, and beat, the vaunted Springboks pack up front. Outside centre Jeff Butterfield scored a try, his third in as many Lions Tests, and added a dropped goal for good measure with full-back Doug Baker slotting a penalty over. In reply the Springbok full-back Roy Dryburgh kicked six points, including a spectacular 50-metre dropped goal from a penalty.

## WEDNESDAY 4th SEPTEMBER 1872

James Magee was born in Dublin, Ireland. The Irishman, who could play at full-back or in the threequarters, represented his country at cricket three times scoring 54 runs. Despite never having been selected for Ireland at rugby Magee was chosen to join his brother Louis on the 1896 Tour of South Africa. He played in 13 matches on the Tour including two Tests.

## SATURDAY 5th SEPTEMBER 1891

The Lions completed their one and only Test whitewash of South Africa with a 4-0 victory at Newlands in Cape Town. All the Lions points came in the second half with top try scorer Randolph Aston and captain Bill MacLagan both touching down while scrum-half Arthur Rotherham added a conversion. Herbert Castens, who had captained South Africa in the first Test of the series, refereed the match.

## SATURDAY 5th SEPTEMBER 1896

South Africa gained their first Test victory over the Lions with a 5-0 win at Newlands. Springbok outside half Alf Larard scored the only try of the match, which was converted by Tommy Hepburn. It was a controversial score that was set up after Biddy Anderson had stripped the ball from Fred Byrne in an act described as "sharp practice" by the *Cape Times*. The match was the 21st and final one of the Tour and it was the only defeat suffered by the tourists. Byrne played in all 21 matches scoring 100 points while Irish forward Andrew Clinch was also ever-present in the side.

## SATURDAY 5th SEPTEMBER 1903

The second Test of the series between the British & Irish Lions and South Africa finished 0-0 at the Athletic Ground in Kimberley. It was the second drawn match of the series and the only time a Lions Test has ever finished scoreless.

## SUNDAY 5th SEPTEMBER 1915

David Bedell-Sivright died aboard HMHS *Dunluce Castle* off the coast of the Gallipoli peninsula and was buried at sea two days later. The Scottish forward won 22 caps for his country as well as touring twice with the Lions. He played 12 non-international matches for Mark Morrison's South African tourists in 1904, scoring a try against Eastern Province Kings. The following year he captained the side on a Tour of Australasia but only played eight matches, including one Test, as a broken leg truncated his captaincy. He was commissioned as surgeon in the Royal Navy during World War One and was stationed at Gallipoli. While onshore serving near the trenches at an advanced dressing station he was bitten by an unidentified insect. He complained of fatigue and was transferred to the hospital ship where he died of septicaemia. The Australian publication *The Referee* said of him: "Sivright was a Scottish forward of the most brilliant type, a hard player, but a clever one. He was one of the finest all-round forwards ever seen in Australia from over the seas and, at his best, was fit for a world's team."

## MONDAY 6th SEPTEMBER 1869

Randolph Aston was born in South Kensington, London. Aston was the star player and leading try scorer of the Lions' first Tour of South Africa in 1891. Aston was a striking figure, 6 ft 3 inches tall and weighing in at 15 stone. The centre had won two Blues while at Cambridge University as well as turning out for Blackheath and the Barbarians. He played twice for England in the Home Nations Championship of 1890. The following year he was selected to tour with the Lions. In total he played in 21 matches on the Tour and scored 31 tries, including two in the Test series.

## MONDAY 7th SEPTEMBER 1891

The Lions closed their first Tour of South Africa with an extra fixture at Stellenbosch. Randolph Aston scored his 31st try of the Tour in a 2-0 victory that completed a 100% winning record for the only time in the team's history.

## SUNDAY 8th SEPTEMBER 1907

Gordon Bonner was born in Wakefield, England. The uncapped Bradford full-back went on the 1930 Tour of Australasia as the understudy to Wales' Jack Bassett. Bonner played in 10 matches on the Tour and kicked four points.

## WEDNESDAY 9th SEPTEMBER 1891

The Lions' first Tour of South Africa came to an end as the team boarded the *Garth Castle* bound for Plymouth. On the field the Tour was an outstanding success with 20 fixtures played and 20 wins recorded while only a solitary point had been conceded.

## SATURDAY 10th SEPTEMBER 1938

A stunning second-half display in the third Test at Newlands saw the Lions shatter a number of records. The Lions overturned a half-time deficit of 13-3 to triumph 21-16 and restore some pride after six successive Test defeats. It was also the first victory over the Springboks in seven attempts and 28 years.

## SATURDAY 10th SEPTEMBER 1977

The Lions played an officially sanctioned home match when they took on the Barbarians at Twickenham in a fundraiser that was part of Queen Elizabeth II's Silver Jubilee celebrations. The returning 1977 Lions party were up against a star-studded Baa-Baas side that included former Lions JPR Williams, Gareth Edwards and Gerald Davies as well as French greats Jean-Pierre Rives and Jean-Claude Skrela. The Lions won 23-14 scoring three tries through Steve Fenwick, Gareth Evans and Andy Irvine.

## SATURDAY 11th SEPTEMBER 1937

John A'Bear became Gloucester RFC's youngest ever captain when he led the side to a 30-3 win over Lydney at the age of 24. The lock had made his debut four years earlier in Gloucester's first ever victory over Swansea. He was to remain club captain for two seasons and during his first year of captaincy the club recorded 29 wins out of 36 matches. A'Bear toured Argentina with the 1936 Lions playing in the 23-0 victory in the only international of the trip. Despite his success with Gloucester and the Lions the closest A'Bear ever go to an England cap was when he was reserve at a trial match in Bristol in 1936.

## SUNDAY 11th SEPTEMBER 1949

Roger Uttley was born in Blackpool, England. Uttley could play anywhere across the second row or back row of the scrum and won 23 England caps between 1973 and 1980. All four of his Lions Test caps came at blind-side flanker and he was a vital component in the 1974 pack that subdued its Springboks counterparts. Altogether Uttley played 16 times on the Tour scoring a try against Western Province Universities and another in the final Test. In 1989 Uttley was Ian McGeechan's assistant coach on the victorious Lions Tour to Australia.

## SATURDAY 12th SEPTEMBER 1903

South Africa sealed their first ever series victory over the Lions with an 8-0 win in the third Test at a sodden Newlands in Cape Town. The match was christened the "Umbrella Test" due to the soggy conditions, which should have favoured the Lions' forward power. However, it was the Springbok backs that shone in the rain with centre Japie Krige, full-back Bertie van Renen and left wing Bob Loubser outstanding. Right wing Joe Barry slid in for the opening try and forward Alec Reid danced past three defenders for another score that was converted by Fairy Heatlie. The match was the 41st and final Lions appearance for England forward Frank Stout, setting a record that would last until 1962.

## TUESDAY 12th SEPTEMBER 1905

Professor George Darwin officially opened the Victoria Falls Bridge, which crosses the Zambesi River across a gorge just below the famous waterfalls. The bridge is 198 metres long, has a main arch measuring 156.5 metres and is 128 metres above the river. Among the civil engineers who worked on the project were Welsh centre Reg Skirmshire and Irish forward James Wallace, who both toured South Africa with the 1903 Lions.

## SATURDAY 13th SEPTEMBER 1924

Former Ireland fly-half Bill Cunningham, who had been called away from his Johannesburg dentistry practice to ease the Lions' injury crisis, helped the team to a 3-3 draw in the third Test. Cunningham danced his way through the Springbok defence from a five-yard scrum for the Lions' try at the Crusaders in Port Elizabeth. South Africa's Number Eight Jack van Druten barged over to earn a draw for the home side.

## WEDNESDAY 14th SEPTEMBER 1966

British Columbia pulled off a major shock by beating the British & Irish Lions 8-3 in a win dubbed the "victory for the ages" by the Canadians. Left wing Dewi Bebb scored a try for the Lions while tight-head Peter Grantham touched down for the hosts at the Empire Stadium in Vancouver. British Columbia's full-back Don Burgess kicked a conversion and a penalty to write his side into Canadian rugby folklore.

## SATURDAY 15th SEPTEMBER 1888

Johnny Nolan scored his second hat-trick of the 1888 Tour and the second in the Lions' history as Hawkes Bay were beaten 3-2 in Napier.

## SATURDAY 15th SEPTEMBER 1973

Two years after playing a part in the 1971 Lions series victory John Pullin returned to New Zealand and led England to their first ever victory there. Pullin was joined by two other veterans of the 1971 tour, Brian 'Stack' Stevens and David Duckham, as England triumphed in Auckland to record a first win over the All Blacks in 37 years. Another eight members of the England team would go on to Tour with the Lions in either 1974 or 1977. Two of those future tourists, flanker Tony Neary and centre Peter Squires, touched down at Eden Park as did Stevens as England ran out 16-10 winners.

## MONDAY 16th SEPTEMBER 1918

The award of a Military Cross to the Reverend Matthew Mullineux, who toured with the Lions in 1896 and 1899, was announced in *The London Gazette*. The citation reads: "He took charge of the Regimental Aid post, dressed the wounded and superintended their evacuation. The Regimental Aid post was subjected to very heavy high explosive and gas shell fire for twelve hours and but for his skill and excellent dispositions, serious congestion would have occurred. His untiring energy and cheerful service in providing comfort for the troops under most adverse circumstances were of the greatest value to all ranks of the battalion."

## MONDAY 16th SEPTEMBER 2002

Syd Millar was elected as Vice-Chairman of the International Rugby Board replacing New Zealand's Rob Fisher. Millar would become Chairman of the IRB the following year after the death of Vernon Pugh. As a player Millar toured three times with the Lions, in 1959, 1962 and 1966. The Irish prop is joint third on the all-time appearance list with 44, which includes nine Tests. Millar also coached the undefeated Lions side of 1974 and managed Bill Beaumont's team in South Africa six years later.

## SATURDAY 17th SEPTEMBER 2011

Lions and Ireland midfielders Brian O'Driscoll and Gordon D'Arcy became the most capped centre partnership in Test history when they were selected to play together in their country's 15-6 win over Australia at the 2011 World Cup. It was the 45th time the two had been paired in midfield and eclipsed the record held by Lions and England centres Jeremy Guscott and Will Carling.

## MONDAY 18th SEPTEMBER 1950

The Lions took on Ceylon for the second time in their history winning 44-6 in Colombo. The local team was composed of mainly executive staff from British companies and the British armed forces with three local players, Summa Navaratnam, Leslie Ephraims and Clair Roeloffsz. It did include one international, prop Howard Campbell had won four Scottish caps in 1948 and 1949 as well as being a former Cambridge Blue.

## SATURDAY 19th SEPTEMBER 1959

The Lions beat New Zealand in a Test match for only the second time in their history with a 9-6 win in Auckland. The victory was just reward for the swashbuckling side of 1959 that had entertained crowds across New Zealand and would have won the first two Tests of the series but for the boot of All Black full-back Don Clarke. The Lions outscored the All Blacks three tries to none with Peter Jackson, Tony O'Reilly and Bev Risman all touching down while Clarke kicked two penalties for the home side.

## THURSDAY 20th SEPTEMBER 1917

1908 Lion John Ritson was commanding officer of the 12th Battalion of the Durham Light Infantry at the Battle of Passchendale. He was charged with clearing out several strongpoints, which included five pillboxes and a fortified farmhouse, near the village of Zonnebeke in Belgium. The resulting action resulted in one of his officers, Captain Henry Reynolds, being awarded a Victoria Cross.

BRIAN O'DRISCOLL (L) AND GORDON D'ARCY

## SATURDAY 20th SEPTEMBER 1924

The Lions went down 16-9 in the fourth and final Test at Newlands as South Africa took the series 3-0 with one match drawn. The Springboks led throughout but failed to shake off the Lions until right wing Jack Slater touched down in the final minute to confirm victory. The Springboks were up 7-3 at half-time through Jack Bester's try and Kenny Starke's dropped goal with Tom Voyce kicking a penalty for the Lions. England wing Stan Harris and Voyce kept the Lions in touch with tries either side of one for Starke. However, Slater had the last word in both the match and series.

## TUESDAY 20th SEPTEMBER 1966

Mike Campbell-Lamerton's Lions arrived home after a five-month Tour of Australia, New Zealand and Canada. Although the first leg had been a success the Lions had been whitewashed 4-0 by the All Blacks and suffered a humiliating defeat to British Columbia on the way home. The Times laid the blame squarely at the feet of the skipper, and management team of Des O'Brien and John Robins, it said: "The truth is this Tour never really got off the ground... the main responsibility must lie with the tour's top brass."

## WEDNESDAY 21st SEPTEMBER 1938

The 1938 Tour to South Africa ended in a 12-7 defeat in an unofficial extra fixture against the Western Province Country XV.

## SATURDAY 22nd SEPTEMBER 1951

The Lions played a rare non-Tour match as part of Cardiff RFC's 75th Anniversary celebrations. Although the fixture at the Cardiff Arms Park was unofficial the Lions side featured many faces from the 1950 Tour to Australia and New Zealand. However, there were four notable absences as Jack Matthews, Bleddyn Williams, Rex Willis and Cliff Davies all turned out in Cardiff's famous black and blue colours. The Cardiff side also featured future tourists Cliff Morgan and Haydn Morris. The kicking of Lewis Jones was the difference for the Lions in a 14-12 victory. Cardiff outscored the Lions four tries to three but missed all their conversion attempts, including one from under the posts.

## THURSDAY 23rd SEPTEMBER 1926

Courtenay Meredith was born in Crynant, Wales. Meredith, who was primarily a tight-head prop but could play on either side of the scrum, learnt his rugby with his village side before moving on to Neath and winning his first Welsh cap in 1953. Two years later he was selected to tour South Africa with Robin Thompson's Lions. Meredith made up an all-Welsh front row, along with Bryn Meredith and Billy Williams, who played in all four Tests of the drawn series. The prop suffered a horrific ripped tongue in the first half of the third Test but played until the finish. And after having the wound stitched twice in the interim played the final Test of the series too.

## FRIDAY 23rd SEPTEMBER 1938

The Lions Tour party left South Africa aboard the *Athlone Castle* a week later than scheduled. The extra week was possible after they changed ship from the older and slower *Edinburgh Castle*. The Lions used the time to play one last, unofficial, match which was lost 12-7 to a Western Province Country XV.

## SATURDAY 24th SEPTEMBER 1955

An injury-hit Lions side was unable to become the first team to win a Test series on South African soil in the 20th century. The team led 2-1 going into the final match in Port Elizabeth but could not hold off a second-half Springbok onslaught. Scottish forward Jim Greenwood scored a converted try to give the tourists a 5-3 advantage at the break. However, the Lions were unable to defend against a barrage of high balls and the home side scored four second half tries, with only a solitary Tony O'Reilly score in reply, as South Africa ran out 22-8 winners and levelled the series 2-2.

## WEDNESDAY 24th SEPTEMBER 2008

Rhondda Cynon Taf Borough Council announced that Dr Teddy Morgan would be amongst the famous people, events and places being commemorated around the area by a series of plaques. Morgan toured with the Lions in 1904 and was the first Welshman to captain the Test team. The wing played 13 matches in Australia and New Zealand scoring seven tries.

## TUESDAY 25th SEPTEMBER 1888

Edward Newman Fuller was born in Billericay, Essex. The centre captained the Old Merchant Taylors' Club but was never selected for England. He toured Argentina with the 1910 Lions playing in the one-off international match.

## THURSDAY 25th SEPTEMBER 2003

Dai Davies died in Taunton, England aged 78. One of three Penygraig RFC players to have represented the British & Irish Lions the hooker toured Australasia in 1950. He played in 14 matches, including three Tests.

## SATURDAY 26th SEPTEMBER 1908

The Welsh duo of Reggie Gibbs and Johnnie Williams shared eight tries as Vancouver were thrashed 63-5 in the Lions' first ever match on Canadian soil. The Lions scored 15 tries in all in an unofficial end of Tour match. Williams added four tries to the 12 he had scored on the main Australasian legs making him the tour's leading try scorer. The Cardiff wing also scored 17 tries in 17 international appearances for Wales.

## SATURDAY 27th SEPTEMBER 1924

Swansea prop Dai Parker's penalty was the first points any side had managed against the 1924 New Zealand team on its Tour of Great Britain and France. However, the All Blacks, who went on to win all 32 of their matches and were dubbed 'The Invincibles', comfortably beat Swansea 39-3 in the sixth match of their tour. Six years later Parker would rejoin battle with the All Blacks on the Lions' Tour of Australasia. Parker played in all five tests of the tour, scoring a penalty in the fourth Test against New Zealand in Wellington.

## TUESDAY 27th SEPTEMBER 1955

Scotland wing Arthur Smith scored five tries as East Africa were beaten 39-12 at Ngong Road in Nairobi. Smith had sustained a broken hand in the opening match of the Tour against Western Transvaal, which restricted him to just five appearances but he still managed nine tries. He would return to South Africa seven years later as Lions captain.

## SATURDAY 27th SEPTEMBER 1969

Wales and Lions fly-half Cliff Morgan was the castaway on BBC Radio's *Desert Island Discs*. Shirley Bassey, Nat King Cole, Hywel Davies and Jean Sibelius were amongst his music choices for the programme. He selected the *Teach-Yourself Encyclopaedia* as his book and a piano as a luxury item. Morgan was the first of seven Lions to have appeared on *Desert Island Discs*. He has since been followed by Gareth Edwards, Barry John, Will Carling, Clive Woodward and Lawrence Dallaglio. The fly-half toured with the Lions in 1955 playing in 15 matches and scoring five tries and three conversions.

## FRIDAY 28th SEPTEMBER 1888

The Shaw and Shrewsbury team took on Canterbury in a one-day cricket match at Lancaster Park in Christchurch. The Lions fielded a side containing three England cricket captains, Andrew Stodddart, Arthur Shrewsbury and James Lillywhite while Arthur Paul had also played first-class matches for Lancashire. Canterbury could also boast three Test caps and the match, which was played for the benefit of the Midland Cricket Club, ended in a draw. The Lions led after the first innings with Shrewsbury top scoring as he made 32 out of a total of 88 while Canterbury could only manage 54. Shrewsbury added 46 as the Lions again scored 88 the second time around but there was insufficient time for Canterbury to bat again.

## SATURDAY 28th SEPTEMBER 1901

James Clinch was born in Dublin, Ireland. The flanker made his Ireland debut against Wales at Lansdowne Road in 1923 and the following year was selected to tour South Africa with the Lions. When he took the field against Western Province Universities in the second match of the trip he became the first son of a Lion to appear for the team. His father Andrew Clinch had also toured South Africa in 1896 with Johnny Hammond's team playing in every single match of the trip. The younger Clinch made 12 non-Test appearances in South Africa scoring a try against South Western Districts.

## TUESDAY 28th SEPTEMBER 1943

Jock Turner was born in Hawick, Scotland. The centre toured South Africa with the 1968 Lions playing in all four Test matches of the series against the Springboks.

## TUESDAY 29th SEPTEMBER 1959

There were 10 different try scorers as the Lions thrashed Eastern Canada 70-6 in the 33rd and final match of the 1959 tour. The Lions scored 16 tries in all at the Varsity Stadium in Toronto. Irish flanker Noel Murphy helped himself to a hat-trick while Ken Scotland, Haydn Morgan, Dave Hewitt and Bill Patterson all touched down twice. It took the total points scored for the Tour to 842, a Lions record. At lock for the hosts was Tom Reid, an Irish international who toured South Africa with the 1955 Lions and had later settled in Canada. Reid played 12 matches for the Lions, including two Tests against the Springboks, and scored a try against South Western Districts.

## FRIDAY 30th SEPTEMBER 1898

The New South Wales RFU met to discuss the idea of hosting a rugby Tour from the British Isles as proposed in a letter by the Reverend Matthew Mullineux. It was agreed that the Tour should go ahead with the RFU paying travel expenses to Australia and their counterparts in New South Wales covering costs once the team had arrived. The Tour went ahead the following year and was the only dedicated Lions Tour of Australia until 1989.

## WEDNESDAY 30th SEPTEMBER 1981

Roy John died in Neath, Wales aged 55. The lock won the 1950 Grand Slam with Wales in his first season of international rugby and went on to tour with the Lions later that year. John played in all six Tests on the tour, filling in at Number Eight in three of them, and scored a try in the second Test thrashing of Australia in Sydney. He played in another 16 matches on the Tour and also scored a try against Manawatu.

# THE BRITISH & IRISH LIONS
## *On This Day*

# OCTOBER

## SATURDAY 1st OCTOBER 1898

1896 Lion Louis Magee played in London Irish's first ever match as the exiles beat Hammersmith 8-3 at Herne Hill Athletic Ground. The arrival of Magee in London had proved a key event in the formation of London Irish and he became an important figure in the club's early history. The official club history says: "Louis Magee's presence together with that of the club's first captain RS Dyas, was to have a major impact… regular fixtures were soon arranged with most of London's leading clubs of that era including Blackheath, Rosslyn Park, Saracens and Wasps."

## WEDNESDAY 1st OCTOBER 1930

The Lions stopped off in Ceylon on their way back from the 1930 Tour of New Zealand and Australia. The final fixture of the Tour was played at The Racecourse in Colombo and the Lions triumphed 45-0.

## FRIDAY 2nd OCTOBER 1987

Keith Earls was born in Moyross, Ireland. The utility back made his Ireland debut in 2008 and toured South Africa with the Lions the following year at the age of 21. Earls played in five Tour matches scoring tries against Cheetahs and Emerging Springboks.

## SATURDAY 2nd OCTOBER 1999

Ireland hooker Keith Wood scored four tries in a 53-8 win over the USA in the pool stages of the World Cup. In all Wood won 58 Irish caps and scored 15 tries, which is a world record for a hooker. He toured twice with the Lions playing 11 matches including five Tests in 1997 and 2001. His father Gordon Wood was also a Lion, the prop toured Australia and New Zealand in 1959 with Ronnie Dawson's team.

## WEDNESDAY 3rd OCTOBER 1888

A 1-1 draw with Wanganui ended the original Lions Tour over five months after it had arrived in New Zealand. The Tour had incorporated 35 matches of rugby union, plus another 19 of Victorian Rules. Forward Harry Eagles played in all 54 matches of the tour, a feat of endurance unlikely to ever be matched.

## SATURDAY 3rd OCTOBER 1970

Lions Bob Taylor and Tom Kiernan captained the two teams as an England & Wales XV took on a Scotland & Ireland XV as part of the RFU's centenary celebrations. Other Lions on view at Twickenham included JPR Williams, Gerald Davies, Barry John, Willie John McBride and John Pullin. The two sides could not be separated and the match finished 14-14.

## WEDNESDAY 4th OCTOBER 1989

A Lions side featuring 11 players from the successful Test series in Australia played France at the Parc des Princes. The match was part of the celebrations to mark the bicentennial of the French Revolution and Rob Andrew captained the side in Finlay Calder's absence. The England fly-half led the team to a 29-27 victory with a try and a dropped goal while Gavin Hastings scored two tries and kicked 14 points. Philippe Benetton, Serge Blanco and Didier Camberabero all touched down for the French.

## WEDNESDAY 5th OCTOBER 1988

Sam Warburton was born in Cardiff, Wales. The flanker first captained Wales at the age of 22, only Gareth Edwards has done the job at a younger age, and led the team to the 2011 World Cup semi-final where he was sent off for a dangerous tackle on France's Vincent Clerc. The following year Warburton led Wales to the Grand Slam and then a successful defence of the Six Nations in 2013. The 24-year-old's leadership and performances earned him the captaincy of the 2013 Lions Tour of Australia, becoming the first Welshman to lead the tourists since Phil Bennett in 1977.

## MONDAY 5th OCTOBER 2009

Johnny Williams died at Sandhurst, England aged 77. The scrum-half was capped nine times for England over an 11-year period during the 1950s and 1960s. A year after making his England debut he was selected to tour South Africa. However, it was the uncapped Dickie Jeeps who claimed the number nine shirt for the Test matches and Williams was restricted to non-international duty. He played in eight matches on tour, ending on the winning side seven times, with one match drawn and he scored five tries.

## TUESDAY 6th OCTOBER 1942

The German U-boat U-107 hit the Blue Star liner *Andalucia Star* with three torpedoes and sank it off the coast of Sierra Leone. The 15,000-ton vessel was on its way from Argentina to Britain carrying 170 crew, 83 passengers and a large cargo of refrigerated meat and other foodstuffs. Three crew members and one passenger were lost. Six years earlier the *Andalucia Star* had sailed to Argentina with the 1936 Lions party aboard. The tourists played 10 matches, including one international, winning all of them.

## FRIDAY 7th OCTOBER 1938

The *Athlone Castle* docked at Southampton with Sam Walker's Lions team on board. The 1938 tourists had been away for almost six months playing 23 matches in South Africa winning 17 and losing six.

## WEDNESDAY 7th OCTOBER 1987

Shaun Edwards was at stand-off as Wigan beat Australian side Manly 8-2 at Central Park to win the World Club Challenge. After a glittering playing career with Wigan in rugby league Edwards switched codes and took a coaching role with Wasps. He went on to join Warren Gatland's coaching staff with the Welsh national side and in 2009 was one of Ian McGeechan's assistant coaches with the Lions in South Africa.

## TUESDAY 8th OCTOBER 1985

Ryan Grant was born in Kirkcaldy, Scotland. The Glasgow Warriors prop was called up as an injury replacement for Gethin Jenkins on the 2013 Tour of Australia. Grant played in three matches on the Tour including fixtures against the ACT Brumbies and Melbourne Rebels.

## SATURDAY 9th OCTOBER 1965

Russell Taylor died in Abergavenny, Wales aged 50. The flanker finished the 1938 Tour to South Africa as top points scorer as injury to full-back Vivian Jenkins gave him an increased opportunity to showcase his goal-kicking skills. Taylor finished the Tour with 53 points from four tries, seven conversions and nine penalties scored in 16 matches that included the first and second Tests.

## TUESDAY 10th OCTOBER 1882

Selwyn College, Cambridge was officially opened a month after Queen Victoria had granted it a Charter of Incorporation. The college's longest serving Master is the Reverend Owen Chadwick who was elected to the post in 1955. By the time he retired 27 years later Selwyn had become a full college of Cambridge University. Chadwick won rugby Blues while a student at Cambridge and was called up to tour Argentina with the 1936 Lions. He played hooker in the 23-0 win over the full Argentina side in Buenos Aires.

## SATURDAY 11th OCTOBER 1902

Swansea RFC got their 1902-03 campaign off to a winning start with a 14-0 win over Llanelli at Stradey Park. Swansea finished the season as runners-up despite the best efforts of wing Fred Jowett, who scored 42 tries to set a club record that still stands. Jowett toured Australia and New Zealand with the 1904 Lions. Injuries restricted the wing to just six matches on Tour and he scored three tries.

## TUESDAY 12th OCTOBER 1948

Johan de Bruyn was born in Reivilo, South Africa. The lock met the Lions twice on the 1974 Tour of South Africa; once while playing for Orange Free State and once while winning his one and only Test cap in the third international of the series. The Lions won a violent Test 26-9 in Port Elizabeth to clinch the series. During one of the many altercations on the pitch Lions lock Gordon Brown punched his opposite number de Bruyn so hard that the Springbok's glass eye popped out and into the mud.

## MONDAY 13th OCTOBER 1941

Mick Doyle was born in Castleisland, Ireland. Doyle both played and coached the British Lions during his rugby career. He won 20 Ireland caps as a flanker and toured South Africa with the Lions in 1968. Doyle played in 10 matches, including the first Test defeat, on the Tour and scored two tries. As a coach he won five provincial titles with Leinster, the 1985 Triple Crown with Ireland and coached a Lions side against the Rest of the World in 1986.

## SATURDAY 14th OCTOBER 1922

Inside centre Harold Davies scored all Newport's points in a 7-0 victory over Blackheath. Davies kicked a penalty then touched down for a try as Newport made it three wins and a draw from their opening four matches. The team remained undefeated for the whole of the 1922-23 season. Davies was called up as an injury replacement for the 1924 Tour to South Africa. He won one Test cap for the Lions playing in the 17-0 second Test defeat at the Wanderers in Johannesburg.

## SATURDAY 15th OCTOBER 1904

Recently returned 1904 Lions Sid Bevan and Fred Jowett rejoined Swansea to take part in the club's invincible season of 1904-05. The season began with an 11-0 victory over Llanelli at Stradey Park.

## SATURDAY 16th OCTOBER 1937

Jack Morley was selected on the right wing as the Great Britain rugby league team beat Australia 5-4 in the opening match of the Ashes. Morley had toured New Zealand and Australia with the Lions in 1930, playing 14 matches, including two Tests, and scoring eight tries.

## TUESDAY 17th OCTOBER 1933

Sid Bevan died in Swansea, Wales aged 56. The forward was a member of the Swansea team in the club's 'Golden Era' of the early 20th century when it won four Welsh titles. He only won one Welsh cap, however he was selected to tour with David Bedell-Sivright's 1904 Lions and won four caps with the tourists. In total he played in 17 matches on Tour and scored three tries against New South Wales, Metropolitan and Queensland.

## SUNDAY 18th OCTOBER 1914

Sidney Crowther was killed in action near Armentieres, France aged 39. A product of Warwick School the forward went on to play for Lennox RFC in Surrey and despite being uncapped was called up for the Lions Tour of Australia and New Zealand in 1904. He played in four Tests and 14 other Tour matches scoring a try in the 19-6 win over Metropolitan in Sydney.

## WEDNESDAY 19th OCTOBER 1988

An episode of the BBC drama *Casualty* entitled *A Wing and a Prayer* was officially released with a guest appearance from Roy Kinnear. The actor was the son of Roy Muir Kinnear a dual international who represented both Scotland and the 1924 Lions at rugby union and Great Britain at rugby league.

## SATURDAY 20th OCTOBER 1979

Paul O'Connell was born in Limerick, Ireland. The second row has won the Heineken Cup twice with Munster, three Six Nations titles, including a Grand Slam, with Ireland and been on three Lions tours. He was selected for the 2005 trip to New Zealand and played all three Tests. O'Connell then had the honour of captaining the 2009 Lions on their Tour of South Africa. When the Irishman was named in the side for the first match of the 2013 series against Australia it was his seventh successive Test appearance for the Lions. Unfortunately a fractured arm sustained during the 23-21 win in Brisbane brought O'Connell's Tour to an early end.

## FRIDAY 20th OCTOBER 2006

Leinster, Ireland and Lions wing Dennis Hickie presented the *Waiting Room* show on Irish radio station 2fm. The 2005 tourist is such an avid music fan that a box in Dublin's Olympia Theatre is named after him. Hickie played in the warm-up international against Argentina in 2005 as well as four matches in New Zealand.

## SATURDAY 21st OCTOBER 1899

Captains Robert Johnston and Charles Herbert Mullins each won the Victoria Cross for their actions at the Battle of Elandslaagte in the Second Boer War. The joint citation reads: "At a most critical moment, the advance being momentarily checked by a very severe fire at point blank range, these two Officers very gallantly rushed forward under this heavy fire and rallied the men, thus enabling the flanking movement, which decided the day, to be carried out." Johnston, an Irish international, stayed on in South Africa at the end of the 1896 tour. Mullins was the elder brother of Cuth Mullins who had also played for the Lions three years earlier.

## SATURDAY 21st OCTOBER 2006

Coach Warren Gatland's Waikato team won the inaugural Air New Zealand Cup after they beat Wellington in the Grand Final 37-31 in front of a capacity crowd of 25,000 fans at Waikato Stadium. Successful spells as coach of Waikato and Wasps earned Gatland an appointment with the Welsh national team. He was one of Ian McGeechan's assistants on the 2009 Tour to South Africa before leading the Lions to a series win against Australia four years later.

## TUESDAY 21st OCTOBER 2014

Former Wales and British & Irish Lions fly-half Gareth Davies was elected as chairman of the Welsh Rugby Union. Davies had travelled to South Africa with Bill Beaumont's Lions in 1980 scoring 34 points in four appearances. He was selected for the second Test in Bloemfontein, which the Lions lost 26-19. Davies kicked two penalties and a conversion before suffering a knee injury during the match that ended his tour.

## SATURDAY 22nd OCTOBER 1955

A rare Lions match on home soil saw the side face a Welsh XV at Cardiff Arms Park to mark the 75th anniversary of the Welsh Rugby Union. Although it was an unofficial match the Lions put out a strong side including 14 members of Robin Thompson's recently returned tourists as well as Wales' Ken Jones, a 1950 Lion. The Welsh XV included the future Lion Ray Prosser while Trevor Lloyd, Bryn Meredith and Courtenay Meredith had all been on the 1955 trip. The Lions won the match 20-17.

## SATURDAY 22nd OCTOBER 2011

England and Lions prop Phil Vickery won BBC's *Celebrity Masterchef* title beating off journalist Kirsty Wark and actor Nick Pickard in the final. Vickery impressed judges John Torode and Gregg Wallace with a three-course meal that included a starter of scallops, followed by lamb fillet with fondant potatoes, and a dessert of orange and chocolate bread and butter pudding with clotted cream. Vickery, who toured with the Lions in 2001 and 2009, said: "I never ever thought for one second I'd have it in me to be champion - who says miracles can't happen?"

## SUNDAY 23rd OCTOBER 2011

Graham Henry coached New Zealand to victory in the World Cup as the All Blacks overcame France 8-7 in the final at Eden Park in Auckland. Prop Tony Woodcock scored a try and replacement fly-half Stephen Donald kicked a penalty as New Zealand won their second title. Henry was the first coach of the Lions to come from outside the British Isles and Ireland. He took charge of the 2001 Tour to Australia that ended in a narrow 2-1 defeat to Rod Macqueen's world champions. Four years later Henry was in charge of his native New Zealand as they whitewashed the 2005 Lions.

## THURSDAY 24th OCTOBER 1912

Scrum-half Tommy Vile, a member of the 1904 Test team, played a key role as Newport defeated the touring Springboks 9-3 at Rodney Parade. It was one of only three defeats that South Africa suffered on their 28-match Tour of Great Britain and France that saw them triumph in internationals against all the home nations and the French national team.

## FRIDAY 24th OCTOBER 1924

Rex Willis was born in Ystrad Rhondda, Wales. The Cardiff scrum-half made his Welsh debut against England in the 1950 Five Nations and his performances as Wales went on to win the Grand Slam earned him a call up for the Lions Tour of Australasia later that year. Willis played in the final Test defeat against New Zealand as well as both victories against Australia. In all he played 13 times on Tour and scored a try in the 30-0 victory over Waikato/King Country/Thames Valley team.

## SATURDAY 24th OCTOBER 1998

Wigan wing Jason Robinson scored a try and won the Harry Sunderland Trophy as man of the match in the inaugural Super League Grand Final as Leeds were beaten 10-4 at Old Trafford in Manchester. After a glittering rugby league career for Wigan and Great Britain Robinson switched codes to play for Sale Sharks in 2000. The following year he was selected to go on the Lions Tour of Australia, where he played in all three Tests and scored two tries against the Wallabies.

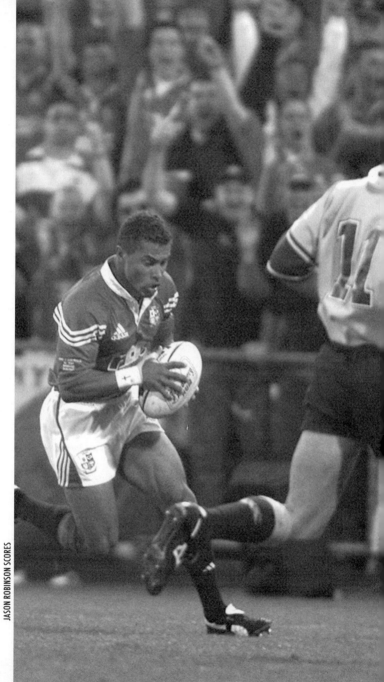

## FRIDAY 25th OCTOBER 1963

Major General Sir Douglas Kendrew was appointed Governor of Western Australia. The former England and Lions prop was so popular in the role that his term was twice extended until he stepped down in 1974. Kendrew, who was known as Joe in his time as a rugby player, toured New Zealand and Australia in 1930 playing in 11 Tour matches and scored a try against Southland.

## FRIDAY 26th OCTOBER 1860

Walter Bumby was born in Pendlebury, England. The half back was one of five Swinton players selected to go on the first Lions Tour of Australia and New Zealand in 1888. He played in 23 matches on the Tour and scored five tries, two apiece against Canterbury and New South Wales and one against Sydney Juniors.

## MONDAY 26th OCTOBER 1908

An Australian side featuring Tom Richards won the Olympic gold medal at rugby union beating England 32-3 in the final at White City Stadium in London. Two years later Richards was playing domestic rugby in South Africa when he was called up to join the Lions on Tour there as an injury replacement. Great Britain were represented in the final by county champions Cornwall who had two 1908 Lions in their ranks, full-back Edward Jackett and scrum-half James Davey.

## FRIDAY 27th OCTOBER 1995

Bill Beaumont's run as a team captain on BBC's *A Question of Sport* came to an end after 13 years and 44 episodes. Beaumont was the longest-serving captain on the quiz show leading his team against opposition captains jockey Willie Carson, footballer Emlyn Hughes and, most frequently, cricketer Ian Botham. Beaumont was flown out as an injury replacement for the 1977 Lions but still played in ten matches including three of the Tests as well as the international against Fiji. Three years later the second-row became the first Englishman in half a century to lead the Lions when he was chosen as captain for the Tour to South Africa.

## TUESDAY 27th OCTOBER 2009

Six former British & Irish Lions were amongst the 2009 inductees to World Rugby's Hall of Fame. Irish lock Willie John McBride, prop Syd Millar and wing Sir Anthony O'Reilly, Scotsmen Sir Ian McGeechan and Bill MacLagan and Welsh fly-half Cliff Morgan were all honoured due to their outstanding contributions to the game of rugby union.

## SATURDAY 28th OCTOBER 1995

Jason Robinson played on the wing in Great Britain's 16-8 loss to Australia in the rugby league World Cup final at Wembley Stadium in London.

## MONDAY 29th OCTOBER 1951

Brynmor Williams was born in Cardigan, Wales. The scrum-half played club rugby for Cardiff, Swansea and Newport but was unable to break into the Welsh national side due to the presence of Gareth Edwards. With Edwards unavailable the uncapped Williams was called up for the Lions for the 1977 Tour and played in the first three Test matches, but a hamstring injury in the second half of the third international ended his tour. Overall he played in 12 matches and scored three tries in New Zealand.

## THURSDAY 29th OCTOBER 1992

Scotland international prop and captain David Sole stood for election as Rector of Dundee University but was surprisingly pipped to the post by comedian Stephen Fry despite having been favourite to land the role. Sole toured Australia with the 1989 Lions playing eight times, including all three Tests, and scored a try in the 39-19 victory over New South Wales B.

## THURSDAY 30th OCTOBER 1958

Tommy Vile died in Newport, Wales aged 76. The scrum-half toured Australasia in 1904 with the Lions playing in three Tests. Vile played in 12 other matches on Tour and scored tries against Queensland Reds and New England. He was first capped by Wales four years later and went on to win eight caps over a 13-year period that was interrupted by World War One, making his final international appearance at the age of 37.

## WEDNESDAY 30th OCTOBER 1991

A Scotland side containing 11 British & Irish Lions narrowly lost out to New Zealand in the World Cup's third-place play-off in Cardiff. The 13-6 defeat to the All Blacks meant Scotland finished in fourth place for the tournament, the Scots' best result in a World Cup. The team contained the captains of the 1989 and 1993 tours, Finlay Calder and Gavin Hastings, respectively. In addition, past or future Lions Scott Hastings, Tony Stanger, Doddie Weir, Derek White, John Jeffrey, Craig Chalmers, Gary Armstrong, David Sole and Paul Burnell were all on the pitch in Cardiff.

## TUESDAY 31st OCTOBER 1972

A Llanelli side boasting seven past, present or future Lions and coached by Carwyn James, mastermind of the 1971 series victory in New Zealand, beat the All Blacks 9-3 at Stradey Park. JJ Williams, Roy Bergiers, Ray Gravell, Phil Bennett, Delme Thomas, Derek Quinnell and Tom David were the Lions playing for Llanelli that day. Bergiers put the home side ahead with a try after he charged down Lindsey Colling's attempted clearance and Bennett added the extras. Joe Karam pulled a penalty back for New Zealand but Andy Hill replied with a long-range effort and the Welsh side held on for a famous win in front of 20,000 people. The celebrations went long into the night and it is remembered as the day when the pubs ran dry in the town of Llanelli.

## TUESDAY 31st OCTOBER 1978

Ireland and Lions fly-half Tony Ward kicked eight points as Munster beat New Zealand 12-0 at Thomond Park in Limerick. The victory is the only one ever managed by any Irish side over the All Blacks. Munster, who were coached by Tom Kiernan, the captain of the 1968 Lions tour, outplayed New Zealand to such an extent that Kiwi wing Stu Wilson commented: "We were lucky to get nil." Flanker Christy Cantillon scored the only try of the game, which was converted by Ward, who also added two penalties.

# THE BRITISH & IRISH LIONS
## *On This Day*

SINCE 1888

# NOVEMBER

## SATURDAY 1st NOVEMBER 1980

1977 tourist Steve Fenwick had the honour of captaining Wales in the WRU's Centenary match against New Zealand in Cardiff. Despite the presence of nine Lions in the Welsh side, including JPR Williams, Derek Quinnell, Graham Price and Terry Holmes, the All Blacks ran out comfortable 23-3 victors at Cardiff Arms Park. Fenwick scored the only Welsh points with a penalty. The inside centre played 12 times for the Lions, including all four Tests, and scored 15 points in non-international matches.

## FRIDAY 1st NOVEMBER 2002

Lions full-back Neil Jenkins extended his world record to 1049 international points with eight successful kicks for Wales as they beat Romania 40-3. The match at the Racecourse Ground in Wrexham was Jenkins' 87th and final cap for Wales, which he marked with four penalties and four conversions. Jenkins toured twice with the Lions and in 1997 the accuracy of his goal kicking was vital to the side's series victory as he kicked 41 points over the three Test matches.

## FRIDAY 2nd NOVEMBER 1973

Johnny Hayes was born in Cappamore, Ireland. The prop was the first Irish player to reach 100 caps for his country. In an international career that lasted 11 years he earned 105 caps in total, the fourth highest for any Irishman and most for a prop. Hayes toured twice with the Lions winning one Test cap on each occasion. In 2005 he played in the home Test against Argentina before featuring in four non-international matches in New Zealand. Four years later Hayes was called up as an injury replacement for Scotland prop Euan Murray.

## WEDNESDAY 3rd NOVEMBER 1965

Scotland and Lions fly-half Gordon Waddell married diamond heiress Mary Oppenheimer at St Mary's Cathedral in Johannesburg. Waddell, whose father Herbert was also a Scotland and Lions fly-half, had toured South Africa with the Lions in 1962 and had met his future wife during the trip. Although the couple would divorce six years later Waddell still went on to carve out a long and successful business career within the Oppenheimer family's diamond empire.

## MONDAY 3rd NOVEMBER 1980

Andy Ripley won the *International Superstars* competition. *Superstars* was a televised competition featuring athletes from a number of sports battling it out over a range of sporting disciplines, including canoeing, swimming, basketball, sprinting and weightlifting. Ripley had come second to rugby league star Keith Fielding in the UK competition to qualify for the international section. He beat off Fielding, Grand Prix racer Jody Sheckter and German football legend Gerd Muller to triumph in the international final. Back row forward Ripley toured with the undefeated 1974 Lions scoring five tries in eight provincial matches.

## WEDNESDAY 4th NOVEMBER 1914

Duncan Macrae was born in Balmacara, Scotland. The centre enjoyed his best season for Scotland in 1938, scoring one try as the Scots won the Triple Crown. Macrae was rewarded for his good form with Lions selection for the Tour of South Africa that summer. He made a promising start to the Tour scoring four tries in 10 matches and earning a place in the Test team. However, after appearing in the first Test defeat in Johannesburg his Tour was ended early by injury. Macrae served with the 51st Highland Division during World War Two and was awarded the Military Cross.

## SATURDAY 4th NOVEMBER 1989

Lions wing Rory Underwood scored five tries in a Test match as England thrashed Fiji 58-23 at Twickenham. The haul was part of Underwood's record 49 international tries for England while he also scored one Test try for the Lions.

## SATURDAY 5th NOVEMBER 1988

1993 Lion Will Carling became England's youngest ever captain when he led the team to a 28-19 victory over Australia at the age of 22. The Harlequins centre went on to win 72 caps and led the team to three Grand Slams as well as the 1991 World Cup final. Carling was amongst the favourites for the Lions captaincy in 1993 but lost out to Gavin Hastings. On the Tour he played seven times, including the first Test defeat in Christchurch. The centre kicked a dropped goal against Hawkes Bay and scored a try against Waikato.

## THURSDAY 5th NOVEMBER 2015

2009 Lions captain Paul O'Connell was awarded an honorary doctorate from the University of Limerick. The second row has won the Grand Slam with Ireland and the Heineken Cup twice with Munster as well as touring three times with the Lions. He had the honour of leading the party to South Africa on the second of those tours. O'Connell has seven Lions Test caps and has played in eight other Tour fixtures scoring one try, against the Barbarians in the 2013 Tour opener in Hong Kong.

## THURSDAY 5th NOVEMBER 2015

The British & Irish Lions revealed that kit manufacturer Canterbury would be supplying the side for the 2017 Tour of New Zealand.

## SATURDAY 6th NOVEMBER 1999

Tries from Ben Tune and Owen Finegan helped Australia to a 35-12 victory over France in the World Cup final in Cardiff. The match marked the retirement of International Rugby Board and Rugby World Cup CEO Keith Rowlands who had helped to make the tournament, as well as the preceding one in South Africa, such a success. As a player the lock had toured South Africa with the 1962 Lions playing in 19 matches and scoring a try in the final Test.

## WEDNESDAY 6th NOVEMBER 2002

Laurie Duff died in Stirling, Scotland aged 89 years old. The lock scored tries in both of his Lions Test appearances against the Springboks in 1938. He played in 14 matches on the Tour and scored further tries against Western Transvaal and Rhodesia.

## SUNDAY 7th NOVEMBER 1920

Graham Budge was born in Hamiota, Canada. The prop played all four of Scotland's Five Nations matches in 1950 and earned selection for the Lions Tour to New Zealand and Australia later that year. Budge played 14 times on the Tour and added one cap to his collection when he appeared in the 11-8 defeat in the fourth and final Test of the series against the All Blacks.

## TUESDAY 8th NOVEMBER 1910

The Tonypandy Riots left property damaged with many shops suffering looting and other having their windows smashed in the Welsh town. The trouble broke out after clashes between striking miners and police. Amongst the businesses left untouched by the rioters was the pharmacy of Willie Llewellyn. However, Llewellyn's fame as a wing for Wales and the British Lions ensured his business was unscathed. He had scored 48 points in 20 Tests for Wales, including the first Welsh hat-trick against England, and was part of the team that beat the Original All Blacks in 1905. A year earlier Llewellyn had toured with the Lions scoring a try in each of the three Test victories over Australia as well as appearing in the defeat to New Zealand.

## SATURDAY 8th NOVEMBER 1986

Jamie Roberts was born in Newport, Wales. The centre was voted Lions' Player of the Series in 2009 for his performances against South Africa in the first two Tests as he formed a brilliant partnership with Brian O'Driscoll. The loss of the pair to injury in the second-half of the second Test was a major factor in the Lions' narrow defeat in that match. Roberts toured Australia four years later adding one Test cap and scoring a try in the series decider.

## WEDNESDAY 9th NOVEMBER 1887

Arthur Shrewsbury's letter to Alfred Shaw discussed selection policy for the proposed Tour of Australia and New Zealand planned for the following year, he wrote: "Amateurs give tone to the team and you may well be able to get them to come for their bare expenses. We want the best of players and a few Scotchmen in the team would I think be popular."

## SATURDAY 10th NOVEMBER 1973

Hooker Bobby Windsor scored a try on his Wales debut as Australia were comprehensively beaten 24-0 in Cardiff. Windsor, who was part of the famous Pontypool front row, was capped another 27 times by Wales and five times by the Lions. He played in all four Tests in 1974 and the first Test four years later in New Zealand.

## SUNDAY 11th NOVEMBER 1888

The SS *Kaikoura* docked in England after carrying home the original Lions touring party who had been away for eight months. However, there were four absences, most notably captain Robert Seddon who drowned tragically in Australia. Also Harry Speakman, Robbie Burnett and Angus Stuart had all decided to begin new lives in Australia and New Zealand.

## SATURDAY 11th NOVEMBER 1967

1962 Lion David Nash's first game as the Welsh national side's first coach ended in a 13-6 defeat to New Zealand. The match also marked the first time Cardiff half backs Gareth Edwards and Barry John played internationally together. In all Edwards and John partnered each other on 29 occasions winning 17, drawing four and losing eight. Their peak came in 1971 when they played crucial roles in both a Welsh Grand Slam and the Lions victory in New Zealand.

## WEDNESDAY 12th NOVEMBER 1952

Stuart Lane was born in Tredegar, Wales. The flanker holds the unenviable record for the shortest Lions career. He played just 55 seconds of the opening match of the 1980 Tour before succumbing to injury. Lane had won five Welsh caps in 1979 and 1980 before being selected for the Lions but a knee injury less than a minute into the match against Eastern Province ended his Tour early.

## SATURDAY 12th NOVEMBER 2011

Ireland and Lions prop Johnny Hayes, who toured in 2005 and 2009, became the first player to play in 100 Heineken Cup matches when he appeared in Munster's 23-21 victory over Northampton Saints at Thomond Park.

## MONDAY 13th NOVEMBER 1916

Second Lieutenant Arthur McClinton of the Royal Irish Rifles was awarded the Military Cross for conspicuous gallantry in action. The citation reads: "He kept his company in hand with great determination under heavy fire, and finally led it over 'No Man's Land' into the enemy's lines." Six years earlier the scrum-half had toured South Africa with the Lions playing eight matches and kicking two dropped goals.

## SATURDAY 14th NOVEMBER 1981

Gloucester flanker Mike Teague scored a hat-trick as the Cherry and Whites thrashed Plymouth Albion 58-0. Teague would finish the season with 20 tries, setting a Gloucester club record for tries by a forward in a single campaign. Teague toured Australia with Finlay Calder's Lions in 1989 and was named Player of the Series despite missing the first Test through injury.

## SATURDAY 15th NOVEMBER 1975

Welsh comedian and singer Max Boyce reached number one in the UK album charts with *We All Had Doctor's Papers*. The album featured the Pontypool Front Row song, which celebrated the Wales and Lions trio of Graham Price, Bobby Windsor and Charlie Faulkner. The three players, who were also known as the 'Viet Gwent', played 19 times as a front row unit for Wales during the 1970s and were only on the losing side on four occasions. Between them they went on six Lions tours between 1974 and 1983 and won 17 Test caps, with Price playing in 12 successive Tests.

## FRIDAY 15th NOVEMBER 2002

The film version of *Harry Potter and the Chamber of Secrets* was released at cinemas in the UK and the US. The adaptation of the second of JK Rowling's novels about a boy wizard went on to gross $879 million at the cinema, the 38th highest total of all time. Martin Bayfield played the part of the young Rubeus Hagrid, the giant Hogwarts School gamekeeper. The English second row also appeared as Robbie Coltrane's stunt double in the other seven Harry Potter films. Bayfield toured New Zealand with the Lions in 1993 playing in seven matches including all three Tests.

## SATURDAY 16th NOVEMBER 1968

Welsh wing Keri Jones made his debut for Wigan after switching codes. The previous summer Jones had toured South Africa with the Lions playing six matches and scoring a try against South Western Districts. After turning professional Jones scored 38 tries in 57 appearances for the Cherry and Whites.

## SATURDAY 17th NOVEMBER 1979

England and Lions fly-half Alan Old scored a try and kicked five further points as the North of England recorded a famous victory over New Zealand at Otley in West Yorkshire. Old was one of eight Lions on the pitch along with Bill Beaumont, Peter Dixon, John Carleton, Tony Neary, Fran Cotton, Roger Uttley and Steve Smith, who scored one of the North's other tries in a 21-9 victory. It was the All Blacks' only defeat on a Tour that included international wins over England, Scotland and Italy.

## MONDAY 17th NOVEMBER 1980

Gethin Jenkins was born in Llantwit Fardre, Wales. The prop first toured with the Lions in 2005 playing in all three Tests against New Zealand. He added another two caps four years later in South Africa and in the second Test against the Springboks Jenkins was part of the first all-Welsh Test front row since 1955 as he packed down with Adam Jones and Matthew Rees. Jenkins was called up for his third Lions Tour in 2013 but was forced to miss out due to injury.

## MONDAY 18th NOVEMBER 2013

On the 125th anniversary of their Tour captain Robert Seddon and the rest of the pioneering 1888 British & Irish Lions team were inducted into the IRB's Hall of Fame at a ceremony in Dublin, Ireland. Three other Lions captains were also inducted into the Hall of Fame at the same time, David Bedell-Sivright, Ronnie Dawson and Gavin Hastings. In addition, Wales and Lions centre partnership Jack Matthews and Bleddyn Williams received the same honour.

## FRIDAY 19th NOVEMBER 2010

Dr James Robson was awarded a Fellowship ad hominem from The Royal College of Surgeons of Edinburgh. The doctor has taken charge of medical matters on all six Lions tours since his first to New Zealand in 1993. Robson said: "It's incredible. I'm not a surgeon and to be recognised by a College like this is just fantastic. In many ways it's the ultimate recognition but I believe it's a reflection on how seriously we treat player welfare and safety in Scottish and indeed British rugby."

ROBERT SEDDON

## WEDNESDAY 20th NOVEMBER 1946

Stewart McKinney was born in Strabane, Northern Ireland. The flanker made his name with Dungannon RFC before making his Ireland debut in 1972. Two years later he was selected to join countryman Willie John McBride's team in South Africa. McKinney played in eight matches, winning all of them and scoring a try against Orange Free State.

## THURSDAY 21st NOVEMBER 1907

Johnny Hammond died in Paddington, London aged 47. The forward toured South Africa with the Lions three times, twice as a player, once as captain and again as manager. Hammond was on the first sanctioned Tour in 1891 playing 20 matches including all three Tests. He returned five years later as captain although he was restricted to seven appearances including two Tests on that tour. In 1903 he became manager of Mark Morrison's team, which lost 1-0 to give the Springboks their first series win over the Lions. Despite his Lions experience and the fact he was also a Cambridge University rugby Blue Hammond never won an England cap.

## THURSDAY 22nd NOVEMBER 1888

Halifax forward Jack Clowes was reinstated as an amateur at a meeting of the RFU at the Craven Hotel in London. Clowes had been professionalised after admitting receiving £15 to buy kit for the 1888 Tour despite offering to return the money. He toured with the Shaw and Shrewsbury team but played in no matches for fear of professionalising his teammates and opponents alike. As well as reinstating Clowes the RFU insisted that the original Lions make a declaration that they had received no money beyond expenses for hotels and travel.

## SATURDAY 22nd NOVEMBER 2003

Martin Johnson became the first captain of a northern hemisphere nation to lift the Webb Ellis Trophy when England beat Australia 20-17 in the Rugby World Cup final. Johnson was also the first man to captain two Lions tours, taking charge of the side on its visits to South Africa in 1997 and Australia in 2001. Lions Jason Robinson and Jonny Wilkinson scored England's points in the final.

## FRIDAY 23rd NOVEMBER 1973

Miss South Africa Shelley Latham finished as the fourth runner-up behind Marjorie Wallace of the USA at Miss World. Latham went on to date and get engaged to Ireland and Lions hooker Ken Kennedy, although the couple never got married. Kennedy, a qualified doctor, toured twice with the Lions. He scored a try on his Test debut in the 11-8 victory against Australia in 1966 and went on to win another three caps with the tourists. He was selected again in 1974 but did not add to his Test caps. Overall Kennedy played in 28 matches for the Lions and scored three tries.

## FRIDAY 24th NOVEMBER 1882

William Cave was born in Croydon, England. The forward was one of four Cambridge University players selected to join Mark Morrison's 1903 Lions in South Africa. Cave played in 19 of the 22 matches on Tour including all three Test matches. He scored a try in the drawn first Test against the Springboks and another in the 28-7 victory over Grahamstown.

## SATURDAY 25th NOVEMBER 1893

William Barns Wollen immortalised Yorkshire's 11-3 victory over Lancashire at Park Avenue in Bradford in his painting The Rugby Match. The painting is now on display at the RFU's headquarters at Twickenham. Amongst the players and dignitaries depicted in the painting is RFU president William Cail, who would coach the Lions on their Tour of South Africa in 1910.

## SATURDAY 25th NOVEMBER 1916

Corporal Tom Richards was commissioned as a Second Lieutenant in the Australian Imperial Force. The Australian-born forward was a rugby nomad representing amongst others Charters Towers and Queensland in his home country, Transvaal in South Africa and Bristol in England. He won three caps for Australia and in 1910 was playing in South Africa when he received a call-up from an injury hit Lions squad as he qualified due to his membership of Bristol. Richards played in 12 matches for the Lions, including two Tests, and scored one try. In 2001 the trophy for the series between British & Irish Lions and Australia was named the Tom Richards Cup.

## SUNDAY 26th NOVEMBER 1899

Ronald Cove-Smith was born in Edmonton, England. Cove-Smith was chosen to captain the first touring party to officially carry the name the British Lions in 1924. The lock's side suffered from a number of withdrawals before the Tour started and a spate of injuries once it began. The injuries robbed them of a reliable goal kicker and a poor Tour saw nine matches lost and three drawn with only nine wins. The Test series was lost 3-0 with one match drawn.

## FRIDAY 26th NOVEMBER 1926

Karl Mullen was born in Wicklow, Ireland. The hooker captained Ireland to their first Grand Slam in 1948 and was rewarded with the Lions captaincy two years later for the first Tour in 12 years. Mullen led the Lions in 17 matches on the Tour of Australia and New Zealand. He captained the side to a draw in the first Test against the All Blacks and a defeat in the second Test. Injury kept him out of the rest of the series as New Zealand clinched a 3-0 win. Mullen returned to lead the side in two victorious Tests against the Wallabies.

## SATURDAY 27th NOVEMBER 1993

Will Carling led England to a 15-9 victory over New Zealand at Twickenham. He became only the second England captain, after John Pullin, to achieve the feat of leading the team to victories over the three southern hemisphere giants of Australia, New Zealand and South Africa. Carling had toured New Zealand earlier in the year but lost his place in the Test team after the 20-18 defeat in the first match of the series.

## SUNDAY 28th NOVEMBER 1971

The Buffalo Bills recorded their only win of the 1971 NFL season with a 27-20 victory over the New England Patriots at the War Memorial Stadium. Amongst the hopefuls that had tried out for the Bills in pre-season training that year was 1966 tourist Terry Price who had a trial for position of place kicker. The Welsh full-back was called up to join the Tour in New Zealand as an injury replacement playing three matches and kicking 17 points.

WILL CARLING KICKS AHEAD AGAINST NZ MAORI

## FRIDAY 29th NOVEMBER 1918

The award of a Military Cross to Arthur Blakiston was announced in *The London Gazette*. The citation stated: "For conspicuous gallantry and devotion to duty. When a convoy of ammunition wagons, of which he was in charge, was heavily shelled and suffered casualties, he succeeded in removing all the wounded men, under continuous shell fire, and by his coolness and initiative prevented further casualties among the convoy." The flanker played in 13 matches of the 1924 Tour to South Africa, including all four Tests and scored a try in the 12-3 victory over Border Bulldogs.

## FRIDAY 29th NOVEMBER 1929

Doug Baker was born in Las Palmas, Tenerife. The England scrum-half toured South Africa with the 1955 Lions winning two Test caps and scoring 21 points in 16 matches on the tour.

## SATURDAY 30th NOVEMBER 1918

William Tyrrell was promoted to the rank of Captain in the Royal Army Medical Corps. The Belfast-born forward first played senior rugby for Queen's University and was selected to play for Ireland in the 1910 Five Nations against France. He toured South Africa with the Lions the following summer playing in 10 matches and scoring a try against Southern Rhodesia. Tyrell would go on to win another eight Tests for Ireland before World War One ended his rugby career. He won the Distinguished Service Order, Military Cross and the Belgian Croix de Guerre during the war. After the war he rose to the rank of Air Vice-Marshal in the Royal Air Force and was appointed honorary surgeon to King George VI in 1939.

## SATURDAY 30th NOVEMBER 2013

Prop Gethin Jenkins won his 101st Welsh cap to overtake Martyn Williams as the country's most capped forward when Wales lost 30-26 to Australia in Cardiff. Since then Jenkins has gone on to pass Stephen Jones as Wales most capped player and has also overhauled Jason Leonard's world record tally for a forward. Jenkins has been selected to Tour three times with the Lions winning five Test caps for the tourists, a total that would almost certainly be higher if injury had not caused his withdrawal from the 2013 trip to Australia.

# THE BRITISH & IRISH LIONS
## *On This Day*

# DECEMBER

## SUNDAY 1st DECEMBER 1907

1888 tourist Johnny Nolan died, aged 43, as the result of injuries sustained in an industrial accident in Ashton-under-Lyne, Lancashire. The scrum-half played for Rochdale Hornets, Lancashire and went on the first Lions Tour of New Zealand and Australia. Born in Rochdale in 1864 he was one of eight children and went on to have seven children himself. Nolan began work in the cotton trade at the age of 11 and was killed after scaffolding collapsed at the Atlas Mill.

## TUESDAY 1st DECEMBER 1936

George Beamish was promoted to Squadron Leader of the Royal Air Force's No.45 Squadron. Six years earlier the Ireland Number Eight had toured Australasia with Doug Prentice's Lions. Beamish played in all five Tests and 16 other matches on the Tour scoring tries against Otago and Marlborough/Nelson Bays. Beamish was one of four brothers who all served in the RAF while one of them, Charles, went on the 1936 Lions Tour of Argentina.

## TUESDAY 2nd DECEMBER 1902

1896 tourist Alexander Todd married Alice Crean, the sister of Thomas Crean, one of his Lions teammates. Todd played 19 matches for the Lions including all four Tests of a successful series. He scored a try in the Tour opener against Cape Town Clubs and another in the first Test. He first saw action during the Second Boer War and in 1914, at the age of 41, enlisted for the World War One.

## SATURDAY 3rd DECEMBER 2011

Welsh wing Shane Williams scored the 60th and final try of his international career with his last touch in Test rugby. The score was a consolation as Wales went down 18-24 to Australia in an Autumn International at the Millennium Stadium in Cardiff. Williams finished his career in third-place on the all-time Test try-scoring list, although South Africa's Bryan Habana has since overtaken him. Williams toured twice with the Lions scoring two of his 60 international tries in the final Test of the 2009 series. He was also a surprise call-up as injury cover for the 2013 Tour match against the ACT Brumbies.

## FRIDAY 4th DECEMBER 1964

James 'Tuan' Jones died in Melbourne, Australia aged 81. The centre was one of five alumni from Christ's College, Brecon, including his brother James and the captain Arthur 'Boxer' Harding, to go on the 1908 Tour of Australia and New Zealand. The Jones brothers both played in midfield and were paired together at centre for the final Test in Australia and the one-off match against New Zealand. Tuan later emigrated to Australia and was introduced to the 1959 team when it arrived in his adopted hometown of Melbourne.

## MONDAY 5th DECEMBER 1898

Harold Davies was born in Newport, Wales. The centre was called up as an injury replacement for the 1924 Tour to South Africa. Davies played in the heavy defeat to the Springboks in the second international in his only Test appearance. He featured in another eight matches on the Tour and kicked two conversions in the 20-12 win over North-Eastern Districts.

## SATURDAY 6th DECEMBER 2008

England and Lions utility back Austin Healey and his professional dance partner Erin Boag performed for the final time on BBC1's *Strictly Come Dancing*. The pair were eliminated the following day after a public vote. The versatile Healey, who could play almost anywhere outside of the scrum, toured twice with the Lions, scoring seven tries in 13 appearances that included two Tests. In 2001, Healey showed why he was known as the 'Leicester Lip' with comments about coach Graham Henry and opponent Justin Harrison, who he infamously dubbed a 'plank'.

## THURSDAY 7th DECEMBER 1905

1904 tourist Fred Jowett scored four tries for Hull Kingston Rovers against York. The wing had turned professional three months earlier and would go on to score 23 tries in 44 appearances for The Robins.

## SATURDAY 7th DECEMBER 1935

Ireland flanker Charles Beamish, one of the 'Lost Lions' who toured Argentina in 1936, scored his one and only international try. The score was Ireland's only try as they lost 17-9 to New Zealand at Lansdowne Road. Playing on the wing for Ireland was Vesey Boyle who toured with Beamish in 1936 as well as going on the official Tour of South Africa two years later. 1938 captain Sam Walker played at hooker against the All Blacks while scrum-half George Morgan also went on that tour.

## TUESDAY 8th DECEMBER 1953

Douglas Kendrew received the rare distinction of a fourth Distinguished Service Order medal while serving as a temporary Brigadier and commanding the British 29th Infantry Brigade Commonwealth Division in the Korean War. Kendrew is one of only 16 men to have received the DSO and three bars, a select group that includes another Lion, Paddy Mayne.

## FRIDAY 9th DECEMBER 1927

Frank Sykes was born in Batley, England. The Northampton wing went to South Africa with the 1955 Lions and scored nine tries, including hat-tricks against South Western Districts and Rhodesia, in 14 matches on tour.

## THURSDAY 10th DECEMBER 2009

England and Lions back Josh Lewsey announced his retirement from international rugby. Lewsey, who could play wing, full-back or centre, won 55 caps for England and was a member of the side that won both the World Cup and Grand Slam in 2003. He won another three caps for the Lions on the 2005 Tour of New Zealand.

## WEDNESDAY 11th DECEMBER 1918

Cecil Boyd relinquished his commission in the Royal Army Medical Corps but retained the rank of Major. During World War One, Boyd had been awarded the Military Cross. The citation reads: "He repeatedly attended to wounded under heavy shell fire... saving a large number from falling into the enemy's hands." The full-back toured South Africa with the 1896 Lions playing in 12 matches and winning a cap in the first Test, which was won 8-0.

## SATURDAY 12th DECEMBER 1908

Tom Richards was among the Australian try scorers when the Wallabies met Wales for the first ever time. Despite the Australian forward's score the Welsh ran out 9-6 winners in Cardiff. Richards was called up to play for the Lions two years later and is one of only two men to have represented both the Wallabies and the Lions. The victorious Welsh side featured a number of past or future Lions including Jack Jones, Johnny Williams, Phil Waller and Jim Webb.

## TUESDAY 12th DECEMBER 1961

Lions outside-half Gordon Waddell, who toured in 1959 and 1962, helped Cambridge University to a 9-3 victory over Oxford University in the Varsity Match at Twickenham. It was Waddell's third Blue in succession and the University's 1961 side is considered its finest ever for completing the season unbeaten having won all of their matches.

## WEDNESDAY 12th DECEMBER 2007

Former Ireland prop Syd Millar was awarded the Légion d'honneur, France's highest decoration, by Bernard Lapasset, his successor as IRB chairman, during a ceremony at Ballymena Rugby Club. Millar was involved in five Lions tours appearing 44 times as a player between 1959 and 1968 and winning nine Test caps. Millar coached the 1974 Lions through their triumphant Tour of South Africa. And he returned as team manager in 1980 guiding the team through a difficult, politically charged Tour at the height of apartheid. As a rugby administrator Millar served as president of the Irish RFU, chairman of the IRB from 2003 to 2007 and chairman of the British & Irish Lions from 1999 and 2002.

## THURSDAY 13th DECEMBER 1928

Harry Jarman died in Talywain, Wales aged 45. The Welsh forward heroically threw himself into the path of a runaway wagon on a colliery tramway and derailed it before it could plough into a group of playing children. Although Jarman survived the initial impact he died later from his injuries. Jarman won seven Test caps, four for Wales and three on the 1910 Lions Tour of South Africa. In all he played 17 times for Tommy Smyth's touring side and scored one try.

## SUNDAY 14th DECEMBER 1941

Lieutenant Paddy Mayne led the SAS on a raid at Wadi Tamet in Libya. Mayne, who toured South Africa in 1938, was one of David Stirling's first recruits for the SAS and pioneered the use of military Jeeps to conduct hit-and-run raids. The tactic was employed at Wadi Tamet with 24 enemy aircraft, bomb and petrol dumps and telegraph poles destroyed. The successful raid helped keep the SAS in existence following some early failures. Two weeks later Mayne returned to the same target and destroyed another 27 enemy planes, after which he received his first Distinguished Service Order medal.

## WEDNESDAY 15th DECEMBER 1920

Ivor Preece was born in Coventry, England. The fly-half is the only player from Coventry RFC to have captained his club side, England Schools and the senior England team. Preece won 12 England caps between 1948 and 1951 and was chosen to tour Australasia with Karl Mullen's Lions in 1950. He played one Test and 10 non-international matches on the Tour scoring three tries and two dropped goals.

## SATURDAY 16th DECEMBER 1882

Australian-born Charles Wade became the first player to score a hat-trick in the Home Championships with three tries in England's 2-0 win over Wales at St Helen's in Swansea. A try was not worth any points at the time, instead it simply allowed the team a chance to try for a kick at goal. Six years later having returned to his native land, Wade faced the original Lions tourists.

## WEDNESDAY 16th DECEMBER 1891

Paul Clauss captained Oxford University to a 4-0 defeat to Cambridge in the 19th edition of the Varsity Match. A victory for Oxford in his third Varsity match would have capped an amazing year for Clauss. The German-born threequarter had scored two tries on his international debut in February, helped Scotland complete their first Triple Crown in March and toured South Africa with the Lions during the summer playing in all three Tests of the series.

## SATURDAY 16th DECEMBER 1905

1899 tourist Gwynn Nicholls captained Wales as they inflicted the only defeat on the 'Original All Blacks' touring party. New Zealand had swept all before them winning 27 matches, many by huge margins and comfortably seeing off England, Scotland and Ireland. Wales won a tight, and controversial, match 3-0 in front of 47,000 in Cardiff. The only try of the match came after a move featuring three Lions as Percy Bush and Rhys Gabe combined to send wing Teddy Morgan racing 25 yards down the touchline for the unconverted score. The other wing berth was filled by 1904 tourist Willie Llewellyn while 1908 Lions captain Arthur 'Boxer' Harding led the Welsh forwards to victory in one of the most famous rugby matches ever played.

## TUESDAY 17th DECEMBER 1974

1968 Lion Maurice Richards appeared on the left wing for Salford as they took on Warrington in the final of the BBC2 Floodlit Trophy. The match ended in a 0-0 draw and Richards scored a try to help his side to a 10-5 victory in a replay the following month. Richards turned professional in 1969 and holds the Salford appearance record, with 605 spread over 14 years with the club, during which time he scored over 200 tries.

## WEDNESDAY 18th DECEMBER 1901

Dr Major Thomas Crean was awarded the Victoria Cross at the Battle of Tygerskloof, when he successfully attended the wounds of two soldiers and a fellow officer under heavy enemy fire. The citation reads: "Thomas Joseph Crean, Surgeon Captain, 1st Imperial Light Horse. During the action with De Wet at Tygerskloof on the 18th December 1901, this officer continued to attend to the wounded in the firing line under a heavy fire at only 150 yards range, after he himself had been wounded, and only desisted when he was hit a second time, and as it was first thought, mortally wounded." Crean was the second of the 1896 tourists to receive a VC after his teammate Robert Johnston was awarded one for his actions at the Battle of Elandslaagte two years earlier.

## FRIDAY 18th DECEMBER 2009

Wales and Lions wing Gareth Thomas came out as gay in an interview with the *Daily Mail* newspaper. He said: "I don't want to be known as a gay rugby player. I am a rugby player, first and foremost I am a man." Thomas' public confirmation of his sexuality made him the first openly gay professional rugby union player. The wing, whose nickname is 'Alfie', toured New Zealand with the Lions in 2005. He played all three Tests and captained the side in the final two after the loss of Brian O'Driscoll to injury.

## SATURDAY 19th DECEMBER 1953

A Welsh side featuring 10 past or future British & Irish Lions beat New Zealand 13-8 at Cardiff Arms Park. It was Wales' third win in four meetings between the two sides but remains their last victory over the All Blacks to date. Lions wing Ken Jones was one of the Welsh try scorers while centre Bleddyn Williams led the side in Cardiff. The other Lions in the team were Roy John, Courtney Meredith, Rees Stephens, Rex Willis, Billy Williams, Cliff Morgan, Gareth Griffiths and Clem Thomas.

## SATURDAY 20th DECEMBER 1975

Lions wing JJ Williams scored a hat-trick as Wales romped to their biggest ever victory over Australia. The Wallabies went down 28-3 in Cardiff to a side boasting not only past or future British & Irish Lions players in all 15 starting positions but four amongst the replacements as well. Gareth Edwards, Steve Fenwick, John Bevan and Allan Martin also scored against Australia.

## SATURDAY 21st DECEMBER 1935

The Mining Society of Leeds University held a complimentary dinner to mark the end of 12 years of service by Professor John Ritson. Ritson had accepted the role of Professor of Mines at the Royal School of Mines, a department of Imperial College, London. The forward toured Australasia with the 1908 Lions; he scored a try in the Tour opener against Wairarapa and was selected for the first Test against New Zealand, but played no further internationals after a heavy defeat.

## FRIDAY 21st DECEMBER 1945

*The London Gazette* announced the award of a Military Cross to Bill Clement for leading a successful raid on a German position near Caen, France despite coming under heavy fire and being personally wounded. The Welsh wing had travelled to South Africa with the Lions in 1938 scoring four tries in six matches for Sam Walker's side.

## TUESDAY 22nd DECEMBER 1908

Abertillery, led by Welsh forward Jim Webb, held the Wallabies to a 3-3 draw. The versatile Webb, who could play anywhere across the front five of the scrum, helped establish Abertillery as a first class Welsh club. He won 20 Welsh caps between 1907 and 1912 and was part of three Grand Slam winning teams. Webb toured South Africa with the Lions in 1910 featuring in all three Tests against the Springboks as well as seven other Tour matches.

## THURSDAY 22nd DECEMBER 1988

Leigh Halfpenny was born in Gorseinon, Wales. The full-back was selected to join the 2009 Lions in South Africa but a thigh injury limited his involvement to a solitary appearance in the 26-24 victory over Cheetahs. Four years later Halfpenny played a starring role in the series victory over Australia. He played in all three Tests breaking the Lions points record for both a series, with 49, and for a single Test, with his 21 in the final match in Sydney.

## SATURDAY 23rd DECEMBER 2006

England scrum-half Matt Dawson finished as runner up in the fourth series of BBC Television's *Strictly Come Dancing*. Dawson and his professional dance partner Lillia Kopylova survived 11 elimination rounds to make it to the final where they danced a waltz, samba and a quickstep but lost out to England and Surrey cricketer Mark Ramprakash. Dawson toured three times with the Lions winning seven Test caps and scoring two Test tries in the 1997 series against South Africa.

## TUESDAY 24th DECEMBER 1985

Welsh scrum-half Gareth Edwards returned as team captain for a special Christmas episode of *A Question of Sport*. Edwards was up against his old adversary footballer Emlyn Hughes in a show that featured celebrity contestants including Stan Boardman, John Nettles and Eddie Large. Edwards had previously captained one of the teams on the programme for three series between 1979 and 1981 with Hughes as his regular opponent.

## SATURDAY 25th DECEMBER 1880

James 'Maffer' Davey was born in Redruth, England. The fly-half made his England debut in a loss to Scotland in March 1908 and was chosen to tour New Zealand and Australia later that year. Davey played in the first Test against New Zealand but lost his place following the heavy 32-5 defeat to the All Blacks. Davey played in 12 further matches on the Tour scoring four tries. On his return to England he was part of the Cornish team that represented the country in the Olympics, winning a silver medal, and he collected his second and final England cap the following year.

## THURSDAY 26th DECEMBER 1946

Herbert Archer died in Bridgwater, Somerset aged 63. The forward was one of four Guy's Hospital players to go on the 1908 Tour of New Zealand and Australia despite having yet to win an England cap. Archer played in three Tests for the Lions and went on to win three England caps the following year. In all he played in 19 matches on the Tour and scored three tries.

## MONDAY 26th DECEMBER 1949

The Gwyn Nicholls Memorial Gates were officially opened at Cardiff Arms Park by his Wales teammate, and 1904 Lion, Rhys Gabe. Nicholls was the only Welshman on the 1899 Tour to Australia and became the first player from Wales to win a Test cap for the Lions. The centre scored two tries in four Lions tests and another 10 in 14 other Tour matches. He also won 24 caps for Wales and captained the 1902 Triple Crown-winning side as well as the team that beat the All Blacks in 1905.

## SATURDAY 27th DECEMBER 1890

Lions skipper Andrew Stoddart captained the Barbarians in the famous invitational side's first ever fixture. The Baa-Baas lost 9-4 at Hartlepool Rovers after being formed by former Cambridge University player William Percy Carpmael. Stoddart had been a member of the original Lions touring party in 1888 and was joined on the pitch by future Lion Froude Hancock as well as Randolph Aston, who would join the first Tour of South Africa the following year.

## WEDNESDAY 28th DECEMBER 1988

Michael Aspel ambushed former Wales and Lions fly-half Cliff Morgan at London Welsh for an episode of *This is Your Life*. As well as earning 29 caps for his country Morgan played a starring role in the 1955 series in South Africa. The series was drawn 2-2 and is rated by the hosts as one of the most exciting ever played. Following his retirement from rugby, Morgan moved into broadcasting with the BBC and his commentary became the accompaniment to many famous rugby moments.

## MONDAY 29th DECEMBER 1930

A proposal was made to wind up the Queenstown Dry Docks Shipbuilding and Engineering Company and put the concern into the hands of a liquidator. The company's managing director was Oliver Piper, a 1910 tourist. Piper was born into a prominent shipbuilding family. His father had been a key figure at the Passage West in Cork since 1898 and had once given Winston Churchill a guided tour of the dockyard. Piper was appointed as managing director in 1917 but the docks were damaged during the Irish Civil War and never fully recovered. Piper toured South Africa with the Lions playing 16 matches, including the first Test loss at the Wanderers in Johannesburg, and scored two tries.

## FRIDAY 30th DECEMBER 1927

John Pring was born in Auckland, New Zealand. The bank manager took charge of five Tests between New Zealand and the Lions including all four internationals of the 1971 series. He is the only man to have officiated all four Tests of a Lions series and received an MBE for services to rugby in 1977.

## THURSDAY 30th DECEMBER 1971

Paul Wallace was born in Cork, Ireland. The tight-head prop toured South Africa with the 1997 Lions and was captain Martin Johnson's Player of the Series. This was due to the way that he, in combination with Keith Wood and Tom Smith, tamed the giant Springbok front row and laid the platform for the series win. As well as playing in every minute of all three Tests against South Africa the prop played in three other Tour matches. Wallace followed in the footsteps of his brother Richard, who toured New Zealand with the Lions in 1993, while a third brother David took part in the 2001 and 2009 tours.

## TUESDAY 31st DECEMBER 1963

Wales full-back Terry Price broke the jaw of All Blacks hard man Waka Nathan as Llanelli went down 22-8 to the tourists at Stradey Park. Price, who was an 18-year-old schoolboy at the time of the incident, put Nathan out of the rest of New Zealand's Tour of Great Britain. Three years later Price would visit Nathan's home country with the Lions.

## THURSDAY 31st DECEMBER 2009

Sir Ian McGeechan was knighted for services to rugby in the New Year's Honours List 2010. There are few names more synonymous with the Lions than that of McGeechan due to the Scotsman's involvement with seven tours. He was first selected as a centre in 1974 and became an indispensable part of Willie John McBride's undefeated Lions. His midfield partnership with Dick Milliken was a key component to the Test side while injuries meant he stepped in at fly-half for the dirt trackers. A second Tour as a player followed in 1977 as he accrued four tries in 30 appearances for the tourists. McGeechan has been Lions Head Coach on four tours, twice guiding them to series victories in Australia in 1989 and South Africa eight years later. In addition, he coached the unbeaten midweek side in 2005.

# BIBLIOGRAPHY

*125 Years of The British & Irish Lions The Official History*
by Clem Thomas and Greg Thomas

*British Lions* by John Griffiths

*The Complete Book of Rugby* by Richard Bath

*Undefeated – The Story of the 1974 Lions* by Rhodri Davies

*The Irish Lions* by Barry Coughlan

*The King Maker* by Geordie Greig

## Newspapers
*The Times*
*The Daily Telegraph*
*The Independent*
*The Guardian*
*The Limerick Leader*
*Wiltshire and Gloucestershire Standard*
*Otago Witness*

## Websites
www.lionsrugby.com
www.thegazette.co.uk
www.barbarianfc.co.uk
www.wru.co.uk
www.irishrugby.ie
stats.allblacks.com
www.gloucesterrugbyheritage.org.uk
www.leicestertigers.com
www.genslin.us/bokke
www.cricketarchive.com
www.rugbyleagueproject.org
wigan.rlfans.com